Testing Is Not Teaching

Testing Is Not Teaching

What Should Count in Education

Donald H. Graves

HEINEMANN
Portsmouth, NH

Heinemann
A division of Reed Elsevier Inc.
361 Hanover Street
Portsmouth, NH 03801–3912
www.heinemann.com

Offices and agents throughout the world

Library of Congress Cataloging-in-Publication Data
Graves, Donald H.
   Testing is not teaching : what should count in education / Donald H. Graves.
      p. cm.
   Includes bibliographical references.
   ISBN 0-325-00480-3
   1. Educational tests and measurements—United States.
   2. Education—Aims and objectives—United States.   I. Title.

LB3051 .G66697 2002
371.26′4—dc21   2002009727

Editor: Lois Bridges
Production: Vicki Kasabian
Cover design: Night & Day Design
Typesetter: House of Equations, Inc.
Manufacturing: Steve Bernier

Printed in the United States of America on acid-free paper
06 05 04 03 02 VP 1 2 3 4 5

For Shelley Harwayne,

who possesses a clear vision for children and teachers in America

Contents

Contents

Acknowledgments

THE IDEA FOR THIS BOOK WAS BORN DURING A QUICK MEETING WITH Lois Bridges in Portsmouth, New Hampshire, on July 25, 2001. We talked for half an hour about some essays I thought I might write. I chatted about how the climate has changed in education since Sputnik went up in 1957. Back then we stressed the development of thinking to compete with the Russians; now we seem to be hung up on mechanical, non-thinking approaches to teaching. Real thinking is being lost. Lois' response was, "When can you have this book done?" I told her I'd write two essays right away and then we could talk final dates. Maybe September 2002?

I decided I would limit each essay to a thousand words or less. I followed the lead (but not the ability) of Lewis Thomas in his collection of essays, *The Medusa and the Snail* (1979), which all relate loosely to medicine and were originally published in the *New England Journal of Medicine*. The essay is a wonderful medium for the forceful exposition of highly focused ideas. Writing essays is like writing poetry—the ideas turn on a very narrow axis.

My first acknowledgment is to Lois Bridges. This is our fourth book together. How many writers have editors who cheer them on? On the other hand, when something doesn't make sense, she is quick with a question. A number of these essays went through many drafts before the main point was clear enough for the reader. I owe the clarity of the text to Lois's careful reading.

I also want to thank Maura Sullivan for her steady encouragement and quick ideas as she read most of these essays. Maura has an unfailing sense of what will connect with readers. Most of all, I am grateful for our regular conversations about life, especially her father's progress after his stroke. Her story about his speech recovery gave rise to "Sharing Power with Intelligent Expectation."

Anna Sumida, a good friend and regular correspondent, has read all of the essays and given both encouragement and helpful suggestions. She has seen the essays in very raw form and followed them through every draft.

Penny Kittle and I are on similar quests, as she is writing essays for her own Heinemann book. She is an extraordinary writer and excellent critic. I am very grateful to her for reading many of these essays and making helpful suggestions.

Sally Swenson and Camille Allen have read the essays and offered both critiques and encouragement. Jane Hansen, though at some distance now at the University of Virginia, has read a number of the essays and responded. As always, I am grateful for what she has to say. Carol Wilcox from Denver, Colorado, has read many of the essays and both sent up cheers and raised detailed questions.

Mary Ellen Giacobbe has been one of my foremost teachers for nearly twenty-two years. I am continually amazed by her ability to extract stories from children. I am especially grateful to her for her featured role in "Everyone Has a Story to Tell."

I am grateful to Cris Tovani, Stephanie Harvey, Mary Osbourne, and Michelle Gallagher for reading some of the essays and for listening to me as I read some others aloud. Sometimes writers have to read aloud in order to feel what audiences sense is right and wrong in a text.

My good friend Don Murray has read a few of the essays and has encouraged me to write more, even a column about issues in education. These essays are more like op-ed pieces. Don, of course, is the master of the editorial, having won a Pulitzer for editorial writing in 1954. I am grateful for Don's counsel.

My wife, Betty, read every word in the original manuscripts and most of the successive drafts. She is usually my first reader. After twenty-five books, she knows my work now better than I do myself. She reads with distance and sound judgment. She is always there for a quick response or needed advice. I will never take her wise reading for granted.

Finally, this book is dedicated to Shelley Harwayne, superintendent of District 2 in New York City, and former principal and founder of the Manhattan New School. I confess that it wasn't until I completed the book that I finally realized I'd been having an internal dialogue with Shelley as I wrote most of the essays. Shelley's unfailing sense of what is right for children, learning, and justice has shaped this book more than I realized. Ground Zero is located in her district. She has listened to the reactions of her students, in print and in conversation, to the terrible events of September 11. She has read the letters of concerned adults and children across the country. I trust her unfailing sense of what is a sound education for children in America. Her influence in these essays is always present. Indeed, she may disagree with a number of them, but that's Shelley, ready to challenge and discuss for the sake of a better way to help children learn.

Testing Is Not Teaching

POLITICIANS OF ALL STRIPES ARE OBSESSED WITH TESTING, ESPECIALLY the testing of reading. Underlying all their rhetoric is the belief that testing will improve reading ability. If scores go up, this must mean that children have become better readers.

Unfortunately, the principle means for assessing reading ability are multiple-choice tests, where children must choose the correct answer. Multiple-choice tests examine convergent thinking. They cannot tell us if the children have read books, related one book to another, or applied texts to their own lives. Worse, the texts children encounter in these tests are often significantly inferior to those written by professional writers. Real authors order their information to engage their readers, and their characters have real personalities, breathe real air, navigate real life.

Still worse, testing implicitly rejects self-expression by focusing on a child's ability to receive information. There is little time left for children to demonstrate serious thinking through writing, drawing, conversation, and debate. Students are not required to use their own words to explicate their ideas. Current testing approaches do not tell us whether students are capable of using information to express ideas of their own.

We forget that writing is the making of reading. Children who write apply phonics, construct syntax, and experience the full range of skills inherent in authoring a text. Writers are more assertive readers and are less likely to accept the ideas and texts of others without question, since they are in the reading-construction business themselves. But writing is very expensive to assess and, unlike reading, seldom evaluated.

The increased emphasis on testing and its attendant promise of rewards has led school systems to abandon the reading approaches that are more likely to produce lifelong readers. Observe the language used to discuss the teaching of reading these days. Notice the emphasis on scores and standards with very little discussion about the ideas that can open the lives of children. We have forgotten the purpose behind reading and have treated it as an end in itself.

Sadly, one of the greatest tragedies of our modern-day schools is the proliferation of aliterate children, who can read but choose not to because there's no real opportunity to engage with books. The pronounced emphasis on testing has created an enormous imbalance between skills and the purposes behind those skills. In short, children repeatedly lose a sense of the function of reading.

Testing is not teaching. Teaching is choosing the right skills based on an astute observation of the child's needs. Good teachers know the interests and passions of their students and know how to put good books in their hands. Testing has deprived teachers of the time they need to teach the skills that will enable children to become better readers. Teachers know that testing inflates the curriculum, that testing itself has become a major subject. Many school systems have three or four layers of tests (building, district, state, national). The time lost taking tests does not include the time lost preparing to take those tests. How can reading, learning, or any other aspect of curriculum be improved if there is such a significant loss of teaching time?

Our politicians believe that all tests are automatically good. They'd better take a second look at assessment approaches, and we'd better help them see both how current assessments are accomplished on the cheap and what full assessment really entails.

The Freedom Factor

A BOEING 767, SILVER AGAINST A BLUE SKY, PEELS INTO A TURN AND smashes into a World Trade Center tower in a burst of red and orange, marking the end of one era and the beginning of the next.

This tragedy brought with it the end of business as usual in America, but it also opened the door on the best that is America, something I call the "freedom factor." The freedom factor is an amalgam of components: initiative, choice, voluntarism, vision, self-discipline, invention, belief in a better way, compassion, and trust in the genius of citizens to solve problems with a spontaneity not born of hierarchies. Indeed, America's response to the plight of the bereaved, the needs of New York, and the effect on teachers and children offers concrete evidence of the best within us. We need to learn from history in order to use this freedom factor in this new era. And we especially need to draw on the freedom factor to establish a new birth in America's schools.

Teachers have always known how to accommodate the freedom factor. I remember the day Mary Ellen Giacobbe brought back to her class some writing from another first-grade class she had visited in Massachusetts. She showed her children how the other children had used invented spelling to assist them in their writing. We laughed together because her children were slightly insulted to think that she had to go out of town to find out such matters. They said, "We'll show you we know how to do that stuff." They did, and an explosion of writing resulted.

This incident didn't occur in a vacuum. Children in this classroom already knew how to exercise choice and use time wisely. When problems arose Mary Ellen would ask the children for solutions. The entire tone of the class was "you are problem solvers, consult each other." But all the time the children were exercising choice Mary Ellen taught them how to use the tools that would make them more self-sufficient. In short, there was a high degree of spontaneity within a very disciplined structure.

When Shelley Harwayne (*Going Public*, 1999) visited her classrooms at the Manhattan New School she expected to see diversity both between and within the classrooms. Every classroom contained a different yet highly heterogenous group of children representing many cultures and languages. Effective teaching meant responding to what the children brought into the room. The variety of expression in writing, art, dance, books read, was phenomenal. And yes, her children's achievement scores were among the best in the city. If you accommodate diversity within children and teachers, as well as the community, then the freedom factor has the best chance to produce what is the best in America.

There have been times in our history when we have trusted the freedom factor in education. On October 4, 1957, the Russians successfully launched Sputnik into outer space. My students were agog at the Russians' accomplishment. A wave of fear and awe swept the country: "The Russians are ahead in the space race. What wrong with our scientists?" President Eisenhower, as if to quiet our fears said, "I am not worried one iota."

But we *were* worried. We investigated how the Russians had succeeded and noted that Russian school children had extensive training in math and science. We passed the National Defense Education Act, and scientists and educators banded together to formulate a wide range of approaches to deal with the problem. We realized that Sputnik was the product of Russian know-how so we realigned our teaching to focus on the thinking behind science and mathematics. Note the emphasis on *thinking*. We stressed active investigation, hands-on work, inductive reasoning.

Our country made great gains in the space race and, indeed, our students began to think. But with the advent of the Vietnam War these same thinking students turned on the establishment, questioned our participation in the war, and sought solace in drugs, the free expression of sexuality, and liberal politics. In the midst of the war President Johnson unleashed his Great Society program with its emphasis on eradicating poverty, especially through education. Unfortunately, as well-meaning as this enormous expenditure of funds may have been, the approach lacked both evaluative rigor and self-discipline. The freedom factor was being exercised but without responsibility and direction. Massive expenditures of money in a short time period without an accompanying sound local vision can go massively awry.

Conservative thinkers and voters rebelled, electing Richard Nixon in 1968 and 1972 and later Ronald Reagan for two terms from 1980 to 1988. Critics emerged from every corner, beginning with Admiral Hyman Rickover, Arthur Bestor, Rudolf Flesch, and the religious right. We no longer trusted our teachers and the students whom they taught. In 1983 our own government attacked public education in a report (*A Nation at Risk* 1983) whose preamble begins: *"Our nation is at risk. Our once unchallenged preeminence in commerce, industry, science, and technological innovation is be-*

ing overtaken by competitors throughout the world. . . . The educational foundations of our society are presently being eroded by a rising tide of mediocrity. . . ." The word *mediocre* was liberally laced throughout the document. The politics of distrust pointed out extreme dangers to national security and business leadership on the world stage. (An ironic sidelight: When the document was written we were in an arms race with the Soviets and lagged behind the Japanese in the manufacture and invention of electronics and automobiles. The value of the yen was greater than the dollar. Today the Soviet empire is no more, and the Japanese stock market is at its lowest ebb in twenty years.)

The top-down management approaches of the business model of assessing the quality of education that arose in the early eighties have gained more and more influence. The standards movement began in the late eighties, soon followed by an emphasis on testing in the nineties, with high-stakes testing the war cry of the twenty-first century. I predict that a standardization of text and methodology will soon follow. As Jay Samuels said on a National Reading Panel video, "We now know the one correct way to teach reading."

In our quest for certainty we have eliminated the freedom factor. The more we pursue certainty, the more suspicious we will be of teachers and educators who are responsive to their students. School systems are already hiring more managers to make sure that standards are observed and that test scores rise. We are well on the road to eliminating the educational methods that have produced the best teachers, who in turn challenge the thinkers in their classrooms. Ironically, many successful businesses have decentralized their operations and challenged their research and development centers to innovate, design new products, and find a better way.

In the aftermath of the terrorist attack on the World Trade Center we have discovered what is great about America, something that has been there all along in our schools and continues to propel us into a position of world leadership. Americans are blessed with the confidence born of freedom to respond positively to problems around them. Great things happen when initiative is in the hands of the individual. It is what the founding fathers, Jefferson in particular, trusted, the intelligence of individual citizens within a free society.

I have seen the fruits of the freedom factor at work when teachers challenge their students to describe the standards of excellence. Teachers, myself included, are surprised to find that student standards often exceed our own. In turn, we need to ask teachers again and again how to improve instruction where they are, challenge their vision, but support them with resources to do the job. This is the genius of America, to find a better way from the bottom up. Let's put our hierarchies aside, trust teachers, and allow the best in America to happen in our schools. We've done it before and, with discipline and great expectations, we can do it again.

Sharing Power with Intelligent Expectation

A GOOD FRIEND, MAURA SULLIVAN, SENT ME AN EMAIL THIS MORNING about an encounter with her father, who recently had a severe stroke. Maura is a Latin and Greek scholar as well as a writer/editor. She writes, "My father and I spent a full six hours just talking. It's still very difficult to understand him. You have to stare him directly in the eye and listen intently for random words to clue you in on meaning, and at the same time not attach too much meaning to particular words. It's mostly nouns and verbs he has trouble with, so conversation is very slow going. . . . All those years of Latin and Greek certainly paid off. It's one big exercise in decoding. And there is a logic to how he expresses himself. It's just a matter of figuring it out."

Maura is zeroing in on the heart behind the message. She knows her father has something important to tell her and it is essential that she remain focused on it. He is attempting to share the emotion and puzzlement of having a stroke and not being understood. Now, at last, the hearts of father and daughter are beautifully synchronized. And this is not a gentle exchange. Maura is frank in telling her father what she does and does not understand. What does come through is cause for rejoicing; what is confusing simply means more talk and translation is needed.

Until recently, I confess, words such as *heart* and *emotion* were missing from my teaching and writing vocabulary. I focused on the head and the intellect. I wanted cognitive evidence that such and such a standard had been met. I'm not saying that I've been heartless in my teaching. I have focused on children and their needs, but an essential element was missing: *the person is more important than the message.* Maura brought all the skill of a language scholar to bear by focusing on her father's halting words, his eye and hand signals, and the look on his face in order to understand what he wanted to say. Out of the interaction of all those variables she caught a glimpse of the feelings beneath the text. Indeed, the feelings were the compass by which she pursued one failed direction after another until there was understanding.

Whenever someone says to me, "He can't even write a sentence," I want to ask, "And what was he trying to say in that sentence that you didn't understand?" Function always precedes form and is closely tied to emotion, which underlies intellect. When our first daughter, Marion, pointed to a bird and said, "Bir," I didn't say, "Marion, it is *birD*. You have to get that final sound." Instead, Betty and I jumped up and down, smiling and laughing in celebration of her entrance into the world of words where we could exchange further meaning.

I remember a time in Italy when we stopped with an Italian friend whose German cousin was staying at a hotel in Lugarno. We found their hotel, had a beer, and entered into conversation. I knew no German and the cousin knew only a few words in English. But with hand signals, smiles, and a very few German and English words we discussed rather complicated subjects like writing, opera, and politics. We used every clue available to us for an exchange of heart and meaning.

All of which brings me to writing as a form of communication. I keep wondering what has happened to writing in a country whose founding fathers prized the expression of ideas in a free society. What is there about writing that brings out the worst in us, that makes us concentrate on the accidents of discourse before reaching to the heart of what writers are trying to say? In 1978 I wrote the following in my report to the Ford Foundation about Americans' view of themselves as writers: "When writing, Americans too often feel like the [ordinary] man who has been invited to a party of distinguished guests. Being a person of modest station he attends with great reluctance and discomfort. He has but one aim—to be properly attired, demonstrate correct manners, say as little as possible, and leave early" (Graves 1978).

Writing has become a pseudo subject. This is best proved in the way we prepare teachers. Most states do not require a course in the teaching of writing, and twenty-four of the fifty state teacher education institutions do not even offer such a course. Teachers are left out in the cold and forced to teach writing as they were taught. The cycle repeats itself again and again, with both teachers and students failing to engage with writing and avoiding it as much as possible. Teachers remain the masters of their student slaves, always choosing the topic, responding with a grade, and seldom reaching in to find out what the student is trying to say. Students, knowing the teacher isn't invested in this exercise, reveal as little of themselves as possible.

Perhaps the problem is best understood in the context of power within relationships. Understanding is best reached when power is shared. In most cases teachers are in the power position when working with their students. They have the power of assignments, corrections, and grades. The best teachers know how to share this power; indeed, they give it away. They are constantly uncovering where the student's heart is situated in the writing. Through the skills of teaching they know how to add power to the student's intentions.

Top teachers I know invite students into the experience of writing. They show the process of acquiring power by using their own texts as examples. They demonstrate passion in their own writing to show its function. They model the answer to the often nagging question, "Why would anyone want to write?" These teachers point up the strong link between emotion and function. Top teachers reach to the heart of what they are trying to say and talk aloud about this search, so that students can witness the process of one's heart coming alive in one's own words.

When teachers search for a student's own meaning in a text, that student knows the teacher's first intention is to add power to the student's communication. When the teacher demonstrates with her own text, the student recognizes the skills the teacher is applying. If the communication is honest the teacher will be as frank as Maura in saying, "I don't understand what you mean here. Would you please tell me in your own words what you intended to say?"

When Maura worked with her father she was willing to give away everything she knew about language to reach into her father's use of nouns and verbs in order to understand what he was saying. She moved into a different temporal dimension. She spent six long hours translating language in conjunction with her father until she could feel their hearts beat in rich, new understanding.

The Greeks have two words for time. One is *kronos,* which deals with minute-to-minute, daily work time. The other is *kairos. Kairos* refers to the fullness of time: *It is now time to plant.* Or: *The crop is right for harvesting.* The Bible refers to *kairos* time in the third chapter of Ecclesiastes: "There is a season for everything, a time for every occupation under heaven: A time for giving birth, a time for dying, a time for planting. . . ." Maura suspended *kronos,* the time she in one sense had wasted in hurried attempts to understand her father, and chose to enter *kairos,* the fullness of time in which understanding could occur.

Good teachers, like Maura, know when to suspend *kronos* and enter into the teachable moment. Power is much more fully exchanged in the *kairos* moment, when both persons are fully present, sense there is no hurry, and know their hearts beat together. Schools and the world beyond them are inexorably attached to the metronome of *kronos*, which wastes the best that is human within us. We need to rethink the place of *kairos*, which pushes *kronos* aside in exchange for lasting power shared between teacher and student.

Everyone Has a Story to Tell

PICTURE A LARGE TELEVISION STUDIO WITH ABOUT SIXTY TEACHERS
seated in a gallery. The teachers are here to observe the taping
of a live demonstration by Mary Ellen Giacobbe teaching
writing to children. Three large cameras are strategically
placed to record her every move. Ten third graders file in, look
nervously left and right at the audience and the cameras, then
sit dutifully at the small tables provided for them.

"I'm sure you've all read some books or heard some
wonderful stories read to you," Mary Ellen begins cheerily.
"What are some of your favorites?" She waits for about
forty-five seconds, the time hanging heavily in the air for the
audience. Mary Ellen is one of the best teachers I know for
allowing children time to respond. They know what her
waiting means: her eyes never leave theirs, her entire body
leans forward in the stance of genuine listening. But no
hands are raised.

She shifts gears. "We'll be choosing some writing topics
this morning. You may have some favorite topics, you have

pets, you and your families have traveled together, or you've seen something on TV. I'm real interested to know about these things. Let's hear about some of your topics. Anyone?" But again no hands are raised. I and most of the other observers are shifting uneasily in our seats. I look at Mary Ellen. Outwardly, she displays no uneasiness, just a relaxed but intent gaze. Finally, Ralph, a thin wisp of a boy, raises his hand. "Yes, Ralph."

"I love my father."

"Isn't that wonderful, Ralph. I'm sure you do. Tell me about your father." Mary Ellen moves closer to Ralph.

"He's in the hospital cuz he had a bad accident with his truck. A guy hit 'im."

Suddenly more hands are raised. A Korean girl tells about the time she couldn't tell her bus driver where she lived because she didn't know English yet. Another student recounts the death of his dog. Soon everyone is speaking, then writing, and finally sharing.

I have replayed that TV studio scene countless times, since it happened nearly twenty years ago. What made Ralph suddenly blurt, "I love my father"? I have seen many children blurt out statements or write things with Mary Ellen that seemingly came from out of the blue. Her physical and verbal stance is born of a genuine desire to know what children know and to hear their stories. That morning, Mary Ellen's physical and facial presence emanated expectation. Her face was relaxed, suggesting that at any moment someone would say something very important. I call it loving attentiveness. This selfless love poured into the space between Mary Ellen and the group. Ralph knew that he was safe in saying, "I love my father," to this woman who was a stranger to him only fifteen minutes before. The spirit of love was accepted and quite suddenly spread to the other children, who began to talk in a rush, each one telling her story, his story.

From birth, children have to be good at answering the unphrased questions (*Who does she think I am? Does he like me? What do they want from me?*) triggered by adults' stance and attitude, not the language they use. They know that what adults say is often unreliable.

Harold Rosen tells the story of a porter at his University in London, England. The porter was a grumpy man who seldom spoke. A professor in one of Rosen's classes bragged, "There isn't anyone whose story I can't get." The class asked the porter to come upstairs for an interview. Five minutes or so into the interview the professor asked the porter, "Sir, I've haven't seen you smile, not once. Why?" The porter replied, "Well, you see, sir, I can't smile. During the Great War a piece of shrapnel cut the nerve in my cheek. Do you know what it's like to be happy and not be able to show it to others?" Rosen's tagline? "Everyone has a story to tell. Will they tell you? Will they tell me?"

Children's stories will reveal most of who they are if they trust us to read or listen with understanding. Every story bespeaks the teller's wish, in some instances the wish for a better story than the one they are now living. Nancie Atwell says, "I try to place writing between where the writer is and where the writer wants to go." But first she has to know that student's story.

I use an incident from my second year of teaching as an example of how we need to tell even the difficult stories about ourselves. David knew all my buttons. He continually caused trouble in the room, but one day I caught him red-handed, reaching to push a pencil into another boy's side. When I challenged him, he brazenly said he wasn't doing anything at all. I was so angry I reached over, clenched the collar beneath his chin, and literally lifted him off the floor. His bulging eyes brought me to my senses. All weekend I simmered in a stew of remorse. On Monday I motioned David aside and apologized for what I had done. "That's okay, Mr. Graves, that's okay." His statement carried both forgiveness and understanding. We had a different relationship after that. Of course, in today's world I could have been sued or fired, my career as a teacher ended.

There is something sacred about a story. When we attend to children's stories, we establish probably the best foundation for their own future as learners. We therefore have to ask ourselves if stories are an essential element in our curriculum. When we exchange and honor stories, we give one another a place to stand in our own small community. Everyone has a story to tell. Will they tell me? Will they tell you?

Let's Change the Face
of Competition

AMERICANS ARE FASCINATED BY COMPETITION. WE WANT TO KNOW who the winners and losers are. *USA Today, Newsweek,* and *Time* portray personal and statistical winners and losers daily and weekly. We regularly take our national temperature. What is the President's favorability rating, how confident are we in the economy, who is number one in the football poll? Businesses compete with other businesses; stockholders want the bottom line to show a profit and need dividends to justify their investments. An aura of finality surrounds these bellwethers. Lose today and life will be over tomorrow.

No question, like it or not, we are immersed in a competitive world. Accordingly, we would like to believe that competition is alive and well in American public schools. Every once in a while we trot out a tough principal who has apparently turned a school around, or we focus on a teacher in a ghetto whose students have excelled. My favorite is Jaime Escalante, the remarkable teacher in East Los Angeles, whose high school students achieved near perfect scores in advanced placement calculus. But for every example of outstanding achievement we cite, there are millions of students who lose out on the American dream. Indeed, economists point to the growing gap between rich and poor. The buying power of the lower and middle classes has been slipping since the seventies, and the percentage of millionaires to the total population has escalated. Economically and educationally, the playing field for America's parents and children is not level. The reasoning seems to be, if children live in a competitive world why not give them more of it in school? Let children be burnished by good, solid competition.

Far more serious, however, is the manner in which children are introduced to competition. We dress them in robes and mortarboards at the age of four when they graduate from preschool and advance to kindergarten. Afraid they will not pick up the structure of language fast enough, we introduce phonics and impale them on initial consonant sounds when they are four and five. We project our fears into their learning and worry that our children will not be in the top reading group or that their early stumbles may signal that higher education will be out of reach for them.

We test our children in prekindergarten, kindergarten, first grade, and continue to do so each succeeding year as our President has requested. As a result, many children experience great pressure, show signs of illness, and in some cases become so fearful they vomit. Children might be able to handle these standardized tests but for the cloud of anxiety that surrounds them. What young children can't handle, and is dangerous to their health, is the look on the faces of adults, the tone in their voices, as they evaluate the scores. What the children see in their teachers, parents, and administrators is tension, fear, and anxiety. Even when a child does well, the tension is ever present. In reality, most of the tests the children take are really assessing their teachers. The district, state, and federal governments want to know which teachers are teaching the children to do well. In many states teachers get bonuses and districts get extra money on the basis of high scores. Don't think children can't tell when we are worried about their position and ours in the great competitive race.

Make no mistake, when children cannot read or write, life will treat them badly. Good teaching is the answer. Good teachers, like good coaches, know how to raise expectations within a learning community. They build on individual power in service to the group in order to provide a level of excellence that transcends what any individual could do separately. Proficient learners help other children become better thinkers. Every child has some kind of excellence to contribute to the class.

Redefining Competition

In his book *Sacred Hoops* (1995), Phil Jackson, one of the great basketball coaches of our time, expresses his philosophy about competition, life, and coaching in this way: "In basketball—as in life—true joy comes from being fully present in each and every moment, not just when things are going your way. Of course, it is no accident that things are more likely to go your way when you stop worrying about whether you are going to win or lose and focus your full attention on what's happening *right this moment*." He continues, "most leaders tend to view teamwork as a social engineering problem: take x group, add y motivational technique, and get x result. But working with the Bulls I've learned that the most effective way to forge a winning team is to call on the players' need to connect with something larger than themselves. Even for those who don't consider themselves 'spiritual' in a conventional sense."

I've watched great teachers like Pat McLure, Nancie Atwell, Linda Rief, Mary Ellen Giacobbe, Paula Rogovin, and countless others. This same spiritual quality that Jackson mentions pervades their rooms. Students are not just reading, writing, or solving problems. Rather, their full focus is on the moment, the immediate transaction. And that moment is the overarching reason for being alive, for being part of this class at this critical juncture in history. There is no learning past to haunt the moment, nor is there any worry about future performance, just *now*.

When these children look at the faces of these teachers, they see knowledgeable expectation born of wisdom and experience. Like Olympic athletes in training, the children in these classrooms put in many hours of concentrated but relaxed reading and writing. Cyclists, skiers, and runners all mention the miles they put in enjoying the countryside. But out of these relaxed hours come pinnacles of extreme competition, the unusual focus needed at the moment they have to deliver. On the other hand, if children feel under *constant* pressure to perform at home, in school, or even at play, they will not do well. The superior learner is not so born.

Current approaches to competition seriously neglect what good teachers have always done, which is to demonstrate such elements as curiosity, initiative, sensitivity to others, and the capacity to regulate oneself. I remember Mary Ellen Giacobbe's simple statement, "Focus on the writer and the writing will come." The top teachers continually demonstrate the function and power of literacy by reading aloud and writing with their students. Children in these rooms want reading and writing in their lives because they've witnessed its power.

There is much emphasis today on the right methods and materials to get the best scores on assessments. John Merrow, of National Public Radio, once asked Jean Chall, "Professor Chall, which would you prefer, a bad teacher with a good method, or a good teacher with a bad method?" She replied, "That's easy. The good teacher with a bad method, because in her hands it wouldn't be bad any more."

Americans had better rethink the learning and competition experienced by our children. So many children are pushed to one side early in their learning careers when they are labeled as disabled or as failures. Standardized tests have built-in failure rates of roughly 18 percent. Instead of learning to compete with themselves, children are asked to compete with all the other children taking the test across the country.

Children need knowledgeable teachers who have high expectations for moments of learning. Continual standardized pencil-and-paper evaluation disrupts learning and causes children to forget what reading and writing are for. The teacher who builds community, a solid team of learners, has always made the difference in children's learning. Let's allow children to see the patient, expectant look on the faces of their teachers.

Necessary Qualities in the Twenty-First-Century Learner

I'VE OFTEN WONDERED WHO IN OUR NATIONAL, STATE, OR LOCAL government keeps an eye on the type of learner we are trying to develop in our public schools. Until we can begin to agree on what basics make up this ideal learner, it will be difficult to consider the best assessment approaches to tell us if our schools are succeeding.

I state the case in terms of "learner" because the evidence is clear that regardless of skill the learner of the future must continually be able to learn new things in the course of a lifetime. The world's curriculum is changing too rapidly; yesterday's information becomes obsolete within a matter of weeks. This means that learners must constantly begin again, transform new information and new skills to their own ends. Fifty years ago, people changed jobs at most twice in a lifetime. At present, many people change jobs (and often careers) seven or eight times, and quite probably a dozen changes will be the norm in the next ten or fifteen years. Such rapid change has much to do with how we prepare learners in our schools.

(And remember, too, that many of the qualities listed here are already under construction before the child ever enters school.)

I certainly hear statements about how students need to be at grade level in reading and math and the like. I've also heard business and community people speak about the qualities they want in the people they hire or the types of leadership required to solve community problems. Meld the two together, specific skills and personal qualities, and a profile begins to emerge of desirable traits in the twenty-first-century learner.

Curiosity. Curiosity is an old-fashioned word that describes the child who moves out to explore and discover. This type of learner formulates questions that comprise information beyond that which she is specifically seeking. All children are curious, but many are fearful because they have been reminded that their explorations usually end in failure. Further, some children do not have adult-learner role models who are curious and carry their explorations to a successful conclusion.

Initiative. Initiative is curiosity's first cousin. Initiative is born of a sense of authorship, *I can write this, read this, make this, do this.* But in many sectors of our society, rich or poor, the exercise of choice can be dangerous or, in communities where children's lives are superprogrammed, nonexistent. We also live in a culture in which we rely on others to provide what of necessity becomes passive play and entertainment. A child's initiative, in work *and* play, is essential to the exercise of curiosity.

Sensitivity. More and more problems in the workplace and community require people to work together to arrive at solutions. Sensitivity means the learner is able to understand other points of view, as well as be empathetic to the feelings of teammates.

Self-regulation. The successful learner must understand her own feelings and then sublimate peripheral demands in order to focus on a desired direction. Unregulated intelligence and ambition seldom result in effective performance. A learner who regulates herself usually has specific goals. The goal may shift, but the learner is able to articulate what she wants to achieve. An important quality in the strong learner is will. She wills her way down the path to solving the problem.

Expressiveness. The ideal learner is able to transform ideas into an artful range of expression. He chooses among the constructs of words, graphics, painting, music, and the like to convey his ideas to others.

Ability to pose the right problem. A learner who is used to demonstrating initiative as a result of curiosity is able to synthesize strains of thought and identify and formulate problems rather than just solve them: *I think that answering question* x *will lead us to where we want to go.* In 1990 the Hudson Institute found that today's jobs require individuals to troubleshoot their own questions, proceed on a course of action, and then evaluate for themselves whether they have answered the question.

Ability to discriminate. Successful learners must know how to discriminate among a wide range of sources of information. First, they need to know how to interview and converse with all kinds of people who know things they need to know. Such traits as initiative, empathy, and the ability to understand other points of view will serve them well in developing this important quality. They must also be sensitive to and able to integrate data culled from essays, books, and the Internet.

When I talk about purchasing a car, choosing a new doctor, or selecting my child's teacher, you can be sure my language will quickly come down to a discussion of qualities. However, discussions of qualities are emotionally laden and sometimes difficult to conduct objectively. Perhaps we fear we will discover emotions with which we prefer to remain unacquainted. Nevertheless, most teachers, educators, and businesspeople can spot the qualities I have mentioned. When we review a child's collected work, portfolio, or résumé we rarely neglect the qualitative details. Instinctively we know these qualities are the strongest predictors of the successful learner in the twenty-first century. It is high time, therefore, to reopen discussions concerning learner quality in the evaluation programs we design.

The Child Is the Most Important Evaluator

How well I remember my first year of teaching. I corrected everything, thinking correcting was teaching. Six months later it struck me that I was correcting the same things in March that I had corrected in September. Instead of teaching children how to read their own work and put myself out of a job, I congratulated myself as a dedicated professional putting in the long hours these detailed corrections demanded. Although I knew something was wrong with the picture, I didn't know what to do about it.

Three years later at a conference in Pennsylvania I picked up a tip from a high school teacher. She said, "I was desperate. After reading the first four papers, I'd say to myself, *Good grief, was this the assignment? Is this America?* It was like we lived on two different planets. I began by having them write the assignment at the top of the paper. Or I'd ask them to write in two lines what the paper was about. That gave me a running start on reading all those papers." I used her tips and added a few more expectations to the student-as-evaluator job description. I didn't realize it then but I'll say it now, *the student is the most important evaluator.*

Current approaches to evaluation have it backwards. At the moment, the most important evaluator is some person out of town who knows nothing of the teaching situation. In fact, the student, who is closest to the work in progress, whether in reading, writing, math, or science, ought to be and is the most important evaluator. The child spends the most time alone with the work and therefore must possess the tools to make evaluative judgments. No question, the teacher does have an evaluative role, but his primary role is to teach the students how to evaluate, how to read their work, and how to ask critical questions.

One year Linda Rief tried an experiment with her eighth graders. She took sixteen pieces written by students in another town and asked her students to rate them from top to bottom. She asked the students to say why the top three were especially good, and what could be done to improve the bottom three. For the next six weeks she continually asked her students to scale their own work, suggest ways they could improve their writing, find redeeming lines in their papers, and so on. At the end of the six weeks she gave her students another batch of papers to read, comment on, and scale. She gave the same papers to some professional writers, as well as to a few top teachers of writing. Then she compared all these judgments. All of her students had made great progress in learning to evaluate; some of her best students rivaled the sophistication of the professional writers!

Rief refined her approach and it is now a standard part of her instruction. She gives the students twenty pieces of writing to put into four categories: 4—Most effective; 3—Effective but needs some work; 2—Ineffective but redeemable; 1—A few redeemable features but much work is required. Then, in groups of four, students identify the characteristics of papers in the most effective category. They also read work of top authors in the various genres and deliberately look for characteristics to include in their own writing. This work continues throughout the year, as Rief carefully prepares her students to be very critical of their own work. (Of course, students can be taught to evaluate in other subjects as well.)

Camille Allen, in her book *The Multigenre Research Paper* (2001), found that students are perfectly capable of spelling out sound, evaluative criteria for their research papers. When evaluation is constant throughout the development of a work, students gain greater proficiency in fine-tuning their judgments and developing new rubrics for evaluation. Allen found, as I have throughout the years, that students' expectations often exceed our own. What teacher hasn't been surprised when asking her students, *Okay, what's a better way to do this?*, to find that they *do* come up with better ways (as long as they think we really want to know).

Learning how to evaluate effectively takes a lifetime. It's all about reading the world, reading texts, reading problems, and, above all, taking responsibility for the quality of our work. For years, teachers complained to me, "The children don't want to revise. What do I do?" My pat answer was "Have a conference with them; talk it over." Inwardly, I knew I was grasping, but I didn't know for what.

One day a student in one of my writing classes said something that brought me up short. She said, "When you read my paper, you see so much that I don't." I replied, "Well, it is always hard for us to read our own papers. We don't have the distance. We're too close to them." A problem was thus identified—how to gain distance, some kind of objectivity when reading our own work. It struck me that there might be a way to teach students to read their papers from a variety of perspectives. I realized there was a lot of teaching to be done to show students how to read their work.

Much of what I am saying in this essay only works if the student cares about the piece he is writing. Several things help students care about their writing: I write with them to show the process, give them some topic choice, have them write each day, and send their writing to broader audiences. I hunt for their voice in their texts (which may only pop out in a single word or sentence), and from the beginning it is up to them to teach me about what they know. If they are teaching me about their subjects, then they are showing me orally and in writing that they have an emotional investment in their work.

I have to respect that the emotions are a big part of creation. Facing myself on the blank page first thing in the morning sends me up and down the stairs for coffee three or four times. I fear that my words just won't come. As a writer, I run the full gamut of emotion: from anger, to fear, to joy, and sometimes to a wonderful feeling of satisfaction. I ought to allow students to express those same feelings when talking about how their work is progressing. Make no mistake, I expect performance and product, but the chance to complain once in a while allows kids to let off steam.

Here's how I help students achieve distance from their work, show their feelings, and develop sound rereading skills. I direct them to choose four papers from their folders (if children aren't maintaining collections or portfolios it is difficult to help them gain a valued perspective) and prepare to make notations on them:

- Put the papers in order from best to least best. Write in one sentence why your best paper is number one, and then write why your least best paper is not as good.
- Which topic did you like best? least?
- Put an S at the top of the paper that surprised you.
- Put a D at the top of the paper that you think is dull. Write in one sentence why you think it is dull.
- Write one sentence for each paper telling what it is about.
- In each of those papers underline the sentence that *shows* what the paper is most about. (You will need to teach showing versus telling if they don't know how to do this step.)

- In each paper find a sentence that is least about the central focus of the paper. (This is teaching students to begin to learn to delete.)

The numbers of ways I can help students read their work is infinite. I may direct them to underline their best and most precise verbs or the best links between nouns and verbs. (If you want some more ideas, review pages 211–23 in *A Fresh Look at Writing*, Graves 1995.) Once you begin to help students with this process, ask them to suggest ways in which to read their own work. Sometimes when students are stuck I say, "Write in one sentence what you *wish* this piece were about."

When I first began to teach, I wanted my supervisors to know that I was hard at work, and the only place I could do this specifically was in my stacks of student papers marked with my red pen. I've long since learned that until students care about their work and are then shown how to read their papers from a variety of perspectives, not much happens to improve their work. Good teaching means showing students how to read their work in relation to what they are trying to say.

When Testing Lowers Standards

I COMMEND THE PRESIDENT FOR SUSTAINING HIS EDUCATIONAL initiative in a country now at war. This is the largest educational initiative the federal government has undertaken since the Johnson administration's war on poverty in the mid-sixties. And President Bush represents the party that at one time wanted to abolish the U.S. Office of Education. Under the banner "That No Child May Be Left Behind," a massive effort is under way to ensure that all children will achieve. Unfortunately, it is at the point of measuring progress that the President's effort will stumble. Standards, instead of being raised, will be lowered.

When large amounts of money are expended on educational improvement, some sort of accountability is necessary. But we need to take a tough look at current assessment approaches to see whether they will produce the high achievement promised for our children. Current tests, which rely heavily on computer scoring, will continue to fail to measure what Americans should prize in their students in order to maintain our number one position in the world. Such elements as initiative and the ability to formulate questions, relate and integrate sources, and engage in good, long thinking get lost in our rush to measure quickly and cheaply.

Parents, politicians, and even educators who have not recently taken an achievement test in reading need to take one. Not until I was in mid-career, when I began taking the same tests and doing the same assignments I gave my students, did I realize how many dumb ones I'd been guilty of in the past. In Colorado it is state law that every school has to have a Parent Accountability Council. One elementary principal called for volunteers but stipulated that council members had to take a standardized test. The parents were a well-educated group and had trouble picking one right answer when they could see that two or even three answers might be appropriate. Further, they were struck by the poor quality of writing in the paragraphs. They became so incensed they insisted that members of the State Board of Education take the test.

Many states have high-stakes testing in which monetary rewards are given to schools, districts, even teachers whose students do well. The effect can be devastating in ways we may not understand. Students in many of these districts prepare for months, taking test after practice test in order to become testwise and do well for the sake of the school and district. Enormous amounts of time that should be spent in teaching are stolen by these preparation efforts, which unfortunately entail handling short-answer questions, reading short paragraphs, and filling in bubbles with the correct answer. Almost all assignments require an answer from multiple-choice options on timed tests. This is the thinking equivalent of the five-meter sprint.

Testing is not teaching. Instead of preparing children for tests, teachers need to teach the skills that will, in fact, make them better readers. Teachers should be giving longer assignments that require students to read, write, handle different points of view, and solve real problems within the disciplines.

Unfortunately, our quick-scoring computers can't handle responses that demand written thought or discern which students can initiate and pursue a long-term project or even read books.

Currently, we are testing what we value, quick thinking. But what about long thinking? Can we discern thinkers like Thomas Jefferson, Albert Einstein, and Charles Darwin, who were self-professed long, slow thinkers? Can we identify and encourage the children who can formulate a question, find the information, design an evaluation, and know whether they have answered their original question? The problems of a democracy are not solved through a single, quick answer but by tough-minded thinkers who sustain thought on one problem for days, months, or years. In short, computers assess very well when there is only one right answer, but fall short when students formulate their own questions or write longer essays to show their thinking.

The strength of our democracy, as well as our great success in business, lies in our capacity to invent, find a better way, look at problems from several vantage points within a free society. I know that our President prizes these aspects of our national character. There is the mistaken notion, however, that a test is good just because it is a test. Current tests require one right answer and are conditioning American children to think this is what learning is all about. The massive amounts of time spent either preparing for tests or taking them have displaced writing and original, long thinking and dulled our students' thinking edge. Current approaches to assessment are lowering standards, and America is in danger of losing an entire generation of its future citizens whose problems may be even greater than our own.

Accountability

WAGGING HIS FINGER AT A DEPARTMENT OF EDUCATION OFFICIAL, the congressman expresses his concern. "Look, we've been pouring money in for Chapter I, tons of federal money, and I simply want to know if we are getting enough bang for the bucks we're putting out. The people want to know, and as far as I can see things are not getting any better." The congressman goes on to say that every business has to show a profit and that education ought to be able to show a profit in terms of better scores. Just as a businessperson wants to see robust profit margins, the congressman wants to see scores rising on nationally normed tests. His key question is, does the balance sheet show improvement in learning?

There's hardly an educator I know who doesn't want to document improvement. But we need to investigate the congressman's point of view, which is really an amalgam of the views of businesspeople, people upset with trends in public education, people in state government, local school boards, many parents, and public school administrators, more completely. Fundamentally, the congressman wants numbers that show that basic skills, particularly in reading, are improving. He believes that school personnel, specifically teachers, need to know that we exist within a highly competitive global market that requires the best in and of everyone. Further, our rapidly changing information systems require an ever more sophisticated labor force. If America is to maintain its number one position as an economic leader, then we must know early in a student's career if she or he is in danger of being left behind, a fate no one wants for any child. Tests will show us if this is the case. Fundamentally, the congressman views the world as highly competitive; accountability requires us to show that funds for education are well spent.

Americans are hungry for statistics: easy-to-understand data to explain a very complicated world. *USA Today* provides a daily spot on the front page for useful statistics. *Time* magazine highlights winners and losers, often in statistical terms. We take constant polls to find out who's the front-runner in an election, how well our President is doing his job, how confident we are in the economy, or which team's quarterback is more efficient.

As much as we embrace numbers, however, we are also suspicious of them. Instinctively, we know that the way questions are posed influences the answers. We prize privacy, individualism, freedom, and choice. We like the underdog who against all odds proves the pollsters incorrect.

Whenever someone applies statistics to human growth and development, there ought to be massive rebellion. This hunger for data attesting to "improvement" leads to labyrinthine state standards and frameworks, with adherence thereto measured by standardized tests. Lesson plans and methodologies are cooked up to match the standards. The computer is an amazing instrument for producing massive amounts of information. For example, at one point Microsoft had taken all the standards for all fifty states and formulated lesson plans that they claimed would meet them. A link stated: "Clicking on this link will initiate a search through tens of thousands of lesson plans indexed from multiple sites on the Internet that match your selected standard."

Remember the paint-by-number craze? Small kits included numbered tubes of oil paint and canvases with outlined scenes broken up into hundreds of tiny numbered spaces. The "artist's" task was to fill in each numbered space on the canvas with the correspondingly numbered paint. The result was a crude, disjointed piece of pseudo art. I submit that methodologies like those being propagated by Microsoft will produce this same kind of pseudo learner. Breaking down skills into their components and testing each component separately produces a by-the-numbers reader who mouths words, not a self-directed reader who puts words and ideas together to produce meaning.

Good teachers know that methods must be based on the needs of the particular student and that choosing a method is an art based on professional experience and a knowledge of the child's interests, abilities, and desires. The objective and procedure exist *for the child*. A physician expressed this same idea in medical terms when she told me: "Medicine is a complex thing, and it is a science, and theoretically the right answer does exist. I've studied and studied through medical school and residency and beyond, but medicine is much more of an art, with only some basic scientific principles to guide you." The art is making the right choice based on the melding of science and the patient.

It seems perfectly logical in a competitive world to have children compete via national- or state-normed assessments. Parents and politicians want to know if children are improving *relative to other children*. A mother in Duluth wants to know if her child can ultimately compete for admittance to Harvard. The governor of California wants to know how East Los Angeles is doing relative to Palo Alto. However, I note with interest that an increasing number of universities are no long considering SAT scores, having realized they present a limited and distorted picture of the learner that does not well serve their university's selection process.

One of the fundamental principles taught in Educational Psychology 101 is "what you pay attention to, you reinforce." For example, pay attention to negative behavior in a child and that negative behavior will increase. We have paid so much attention to numerical scores that our appetite craves only more scores—and testing companies are only too happy to use computers to deliver these disaggregated scores as only computers can. One day we will discover, as many universities already have, that what we've been evaluating isn't worth evaluating at all. Normed assessments tied to high-stakes rewards have turned teachers' attention away from what should be their primary concerns—expressive ability, long thinking, and skilled integration of learning into life. Such abilities are not assessed, because doing so is too expensive and because it is extremely difficult to compare them across populations. But does a particular ability or skill become less important just because it cannot be tested effectively?

"All right," say the legislators, the businesspeople, the parents, "If not normed assessments, then what do you suggest that will keep our schools accountable?" I do believe in accountability. Therefore, many of us had better stop complaining and come up with alternative approaches to assessment that are instructionally rewarding and come closest to what teachers should be doing day after day in their classroom. We can keep some elements of assessment that lend themselves to standardized approaches, but much more funding needs to go into creating far more challenging procedures.

A Pessimist Looks at the Future
of Education in America

I'M NOT NORMALLY A PESSIMISTIC PERSON. I SEE OPENINGS AND possibilities in most every problem. But I have found my optimism about the future of education eroding in recent years. I worry about a country in which greed replaces outrage over injustice. We preach freedom to other countries, forgetting that the growing imbalance between rich and poor at home gives our voice a decidedly tinny ring on the international scene. Freedom is not a birthright. Rather, it must be won by each generation. And it is principally won by helping others to be free and to have a future within our democracy.

A rank materialism makes us focus on "getting ours" even at the expense of our neighbors, our friends, and especially our children. Multibillion-dollar media campaigns are waged to convince us we need more than we do. Sadly, children begin to focus on extrinsic motivations in their crib. They learn that personal satisfaction is derived from material goods, television, rewards given and withheld. Personal satisfaction derived from one's own actions is buried under an avalanche of created need, to the point of being paid for good grades. Learning for its own sake is lost.

For one brief moment following September 11, 2001, we saw ourselves in the mirror and were pulled up short. We didn't like our materialism pursued at the expense of our children and loved ones. We embraced our families, went to church, and sang "America the Beautiful" with fervor. By mid-December all that remained were a few fluttering flags. Constitution scholar Seymour Lipsett (1996) points out that Americans are very good at responding to crises but are simply unable to sustain efforts for the long haul or to plan to avoid future crises.

"Getting ours" seriously undermines public education, the bulwark of a democracy. Politicians and businesspeople have convinced the public that education is in a sorry state, worse than in the past. There *are* problems in education, but the crisis has mainly been manufactured (see Berliner and Biddle, *The Manufactured Crisis,* 1995). What you pay attention to, you reinforce. More and more parents are removing their children to the sanctity of private campuses because they can afford to. Families not of means pray for scholarships to elite institutions. Our aging population of baby boomers is less willing to invest in public school children, the future of the nation. Money for public education is in increasingly short supply. We spend billions on toys and designer clothing for our children and complain bitterly about the taxes used to help them learn to be able to contribute to a democratic society. Court case after court case seeks to divert public money to private education.

Good teachers, more than methods and materials, make the difference in our children's learning. As money for education dries up, how will our classrooms be able to compete for the best and brightest professionals? Our children have less and less access to well-prepared teachers. High stress raises absenteeism. Many substitutes are not certified, and an even larger number have never taught. Worse, the dropout rate of new teachers in their first three years of teaching is soaring. To combat the shortage most states offer alternative certifications. The necessary background courses in human development, learning theory, and curriculum instruction are often bypassed. Students have teachers who are highly susceptible to method-oriented teaching packages rather than those who teach in response to student needs.

Professional control in the classroom continues to lessen, and the role of supervisors continues to increase. Decisions once made locally are being made further and further from the teacher-child transaction. We used to say, "Close the door and teach according to your best professional judgment." But the teacher can't close the door on prescribed materials, methodologies, and evaluations. It is difficult to break away from a mandated package that results in public disclosure of test scores by building and room and is tied to salary increments.

I am pessimistic because in a world in which teachers must adapt their instruction to an increasingly complex range of emotional and intellectual needs, the unique emotional needs of individual children are bypassed in the rush to cover curriculum. Human beings are not products or quantities. Emotion is the engine of the intellect. A child's interest is piqued by a story about a boy and his dog. Yearning for this feeling of companionship, he reads the story and in the process learns about love and responsibility. In turn, the intellect feeds the joy of learning. Intellect and emotion are synergistic. Teachers who know their children well instinctively capitalize on their emotions to lead them to greater learning.

I am also pessimistic because the voices of educators at such revered institutions as Harvard, Brown, and Stanford are not more forthright in commanding attention on the national scene. Forty years ago we had educators whose opinions and research mattered, people like John Gardiner, Harold Howe, Jerome Bruner, and even President Conant of Harvard. The country's best minds grappled with education as an entity, and student thinking was emphasized. Admittedly, we were concerned about the Russians outperforming us in science and mathematics.

Where are our great minds in education today? Who is stepping up to the plate to produce the critiques and make the proposals that challenge our minds in the fullest sense? A few lone voices like Alfie Kohn, Susan Ohanian, Ken Goodman, Elaine Garan, and Richard Allington battle the elements of entrenchment and propose imaginative, humane alternatives that are grounded in recapturing the fire of democracy for the education of all the people.

I am most unhappy as I write this essay. I fear we have lost the challenge of the Declaration of Independence in our anxieties over dividends based on the bottom line, profit. Yes, profit before people. Personal greed before a concern for others. I fear for the future of my grandchildren, and their children's children.

Assessments That Raise Standards

AMERICA HAS LONG EMBRACED THE PRIMACY OF LOCAL CONTROL OF education. That is, it is up to the local school board to make decisions about what is qualitatively best for the community's children. Increasingly, however, states and even the federal government have usurped local control by constructing state curriculum frameworks tied to required standardized assessments. True, most Americans want to know how local students compare with others across the country. And there is much evidence to show that not all communities have had high enough expectations for their students and that local curriculum doesn't always measure up to what students need to survive in a complex, skill-oriented world. The standardized assessment has thus become the means to compare one school system with another. Students undergo extensive assessments to let parents, politicians, and local educators know how they are doing.

Whenever standards are determined away from the local arena and normed tests are used to assess those standards, compromises are made in test design that highlight certain aspects of learning and literacy over others. Whatever can be more cheaply and easily scored by computer tends to be emphasized in instruction. Given the rewards attached to high-stakes testing, it is only natural that schools will try to match instruction to the test rather than emphasize qualities that contribute to longer-lasting learning. For example, initiative, self-regulation, will, and the ability to identify and formulate problems cannot be assessed by a multiple-choice test. More and more assessments are drifting farther and further away from what strong teachers actually do when they teach children to read and write.

I am a bitter critic of standardized assessments, believing strongly as I do that they lower standards instead of raising them. Current approaches to standardized assessment in both reading and writing have little to do with how either is or ought to be taught.

It is easy to criticize; proposing an alternative is far more difficult. Nevertheless, here's an outline for an alternative approach to assessing the literacy abilities and qualities we expect to see in the twenty-first-century learner. Above all, we want the obvious function of reading and writing to be evident in the assessments. Students should be reading well-written books by professional authors. They ought to be required, with teacher help, to initiate reading books and composing texts on topics they wish to know more about.

A Proposal for an Alternative Assessment in Reading

This alternative proposal is especially geared to assess student performance in several areas: knowledge of phonics, ability to read and comprehend paragraphs written in a variety of genres, and the actual reading of books. Until the reading of books is included in assessment, there is no proof that the skills normally measured by standardized assessments have any validity. Sadly, one of the major gaps in our assessments is in determining which students read books and apply the contents to their own lives. One of the major problems we have in the teaching of reading is the *aliterate* reader, a reader who can read but doesn't. Until students read on their own, books have not become a part of their lives and the function of reading has not been understood.

I propose that students present a list of at least ten books they have read, to include some at each of three levels of difficulty: easy (below grade level), at grade level, and challenging. The books ought to be in a variety of genres, or at least include fiction and nonfiction. It is up to the student, working with the teacher, to select good books to read and to be the prime initiator of reading.

Teachers will then choose three books from the ten to use to evaluate the student for (1) comprehension of text as it relates to detailed understanding, (2) ability to relate text to life, (3) ability to relate the book to other books read, and (4) the overall relevance of books to him or her. Teachers will record handwritten evidence in each of the assessment areas and make evaluative judgments in each category. This assessment can be based on a combination of both oral and written work by the student, depending on age.

Traditional standardized assessments will also be administered with regard to basic word skills and the ability to comprehend short paragraphs, but the informal trade book inventory must have substantial weight in the overall evaluation of the student's status as a reader.

Schools who wish to be successful with this approach to evaluation must provide a rich array of books for children to read. Jeff McQuillan (1998) has shown the high correlation between reading performance and book accessibility. A fringe benefit is that the literacy of the faculty will rise as well simply because they too will read these books and constantly interpret reading abilities within a much broader field.

A Proposal for an Alternative Assessment of Writing

Most writers I know prepare for their writing. That is, they may do some reading, conduct some interviews with authorities on the topic, or bounce ideas off colleagues. The prepared mind creates much more interesting texts, both for the writer and for the reader.

Current approaches to assessing writing usually provide a single prompt: "Write about an interesting experience in your life," or "Write a letter to a company about something you would like to buy." The main reason for having a single stimulus like this is that it makes scoring easier: reviewers can decide rather quickly where the student falls within the rubrics of fluency, use of details, coherence, use of conventions, and so on.

A far more demanding yet fairer approach, for both students and teachers, is to have students write on a topic that interests them and on which they have already prepared their ideas and marshaled their thinking by reading and turning possibilities over in their minds. They might even have practiced a first draft. Such a test would certainly be fairer to students who need more time to get their thoughts in order or who come from another culture. Further, giving the student responsibility for conscious preparation mirrors the instructional situation.

Here's how it works. From September to May children conduct interviews and chat about various areas of interest. Their task is to build a list of special interests and personal experiences. They may explore fiction, develop certain characters, and write poetry on these topics. Depending on the age of the children, they then present five, six, or seven topics on which they feel qualified to write. Throughout the year the teacher shows the student how to develop a good list. Two- or three-sentence descriptions accompany the topics on the list. Finally, in May, the teacher selects two items from the list on which the student writes, in a genre specified by the teacher. Teachers who review these exams will find doing so much closer to their day-to-day teaching.

Placing too much store in comparing populations with normed assessments causes us to bypass more demanding local reviews of student reading and writing. America has fallen in love with numbers that we believe give us reliable data about the status of current affairs. Education, especially in relation to assessment, has not escaped this tendency. Unfortunately, the gradual drift away from local initiative, student and teacher responsibility, and the assessment of characteristics of the perceptive, divergent thinker are being lost. We need to reexamine this drift before our position as a world leader is also lost.

Tap Teacher Expertise for Higher Standards

TEACHER JUDGMENT HAS BEEN BYPASSED IN OUR RUSH TO RAISE standards in American education. In 1990 panels of experts, among them representatives of the National Council of Teachers of English and the International Reading Association, were asked to develop standards. Certainly, these panels knew something about what the good reading or writing student should be able to do. And they did consult many teachers, some of whom pilot-tested the standards and portfolios. Fashioning the final statements of standards took several years, but under no little time pressure they were duly delivered. In turn, states bought into what the "experts" said and chose those standards that fit their various situations. And that was the end of that.

Unfortunately, no one foresaw how the standards would be misused. Instead of being seen as goals or guidelines, they were pressed into service with the expectation that teachers would drop what they were doing and make major shifts in their current practice. Standards only work when they are developed locally and implemented with enough inservice support to allow real change to take place.

Standards from out of town can perhaps be useful as general guidelines stated as goals. Standards developed from afar tend to be abstract and leave out local aspirations, the real energy behind successful change. Energy developed at the national or state level tends to be so diluted when it reaches local school systems and classrooms that teachers soon see the standard as an imposition rather than an opportunity. The mood in the trenches quickly shifts from enthusiasm to obstinate resistance when teachers' decisions are questioned or they are told they aren't implementing change quickly enough to placate the politicians.

Let me make an analogy here. In the late fifties and early sixties, Japanese industry was taking careful note of the steel and auto industry in America. They took what they'd learned about better production methods, but then *transformed the means for implementing* these methods. In no time they realized that the worker on the line, the one closest to hands-on production, knew things middle management had not yet learned. They created quality circles in which middle management and workers sat around the same table and discussed the best way to improve production. In many cases executive offices were abolished in favor of the conference room. It wasn't long before the Japanese auto industry overtook our own and forged ahead in both quality and output. Where had we gone wrong? A large middle management component in our auto industry was sapping extra dollars from both profits and production. Middle management's job in our production design was to maintain quality control, but the managers were sitting in offices far away from the production line. Ironically, the workers on the line saw quality in production as the manager's job, not their own. Our automakers responded slowly but eventually paid more attention to the workers on the line.

We in education are mirroring the U.S. auto industry in the fifties with our top-down management structures that remove quality control from those who understand what goes on day to day in the classroom. Majors and generals who sit in headquarters far to the rear and receive little communication from the foot soldiers in the middle of the action can overly simplify solutions. Any stance an official takes can seem perfectly logical when separated from the response of those involved in that stance's day-to-day implementation. On the other hand, when administrators provide resources that support what teachers see as essential to better teaching, long-term change is the result.

Teachers are buried in an avalanche of expectations: standards, testing, and expanded curricula. The expectations come from every level of government and administration as well as from parents and the community. They are rarely part of a long-term plan carefully developed in conjunction with the teachers. Rather, these expectations demand immediate response, and no attempt is made to monitor their effect on the classroom. In our insane preoccupation with test scores, we have failed to conduct research where it is most needed, *in the classroom*. We need time/space studies of and by real teachers in order to see if our expectations are remotely realistic.

Consider the layering of expectations in one New England state. There are twelve standards for teacher-preparing institutions, with seven indicators or subcategories for each. When professors teach, they must write out the specific standard so students will know which of the twelve is being addressed. Of course, some lessons will draw on three or four standards simultaneously. Standards will be reviewed and new ones introduced in the same class. Classroom teachers in this state must also follow state standards or frameworks. Their plans must show which standard is being taught. Papers mounted on the bulletin board must have the relevant state standard prominently labeled above them. Visitors or supervisors who come into the classroom immediately ask both the teacher and the children which standard is the focus of instruction.

The assumption in such a hierarchical framework is that the persons highest in the chain of command possess more wisdom than the persons below. Each level of management demands more discrete evidence that standards are being followed, until the classroom teacher is left with little intelligent discretion. My greatest concern is that teachers will look up to the "wisdom" of power and authority instead of down to the children who are the source of what needs to be taught. When responsive teachers find that today's lesson works for four of their students but not for six others, they adjust their instruction on the spot. A good science lesson may explicate four or five standards simultaneously, as adjusted for linguistic and cultural differences.

Susan Ohanian's *One Size Fits Few: The Folly of Educational Standards* (2000) details the fallacy of the standards movement for teachers who are sensitive to their students' needs. The best teachers I know, whose students produce exemplary work, have individual expectations for each student. What they may have stated as a direction is changed one, two, or three times in the space of an hour. This is the reflective practitioner at work. Unfortunately, reflective practitioners are the ones most disturbed by the current rush to standardization. They know instinctively that a standardized methodology bypasses real thinking to produce one-dimensional, cookie-cutter kids.

Clearly, the amount of effort that has gone and continues to go into the standards movement is substantial. There is very little time within the daily crunch of bells and lessons and field trips and scraped knees for data to travel up through the hierarchy to reach decision makers. There is *already* a predetermined view of the profile of success, so why is informed response needed? Classroom performance matches standards or it doesn't. But the teacher is closest to the student and usually knows what works.

Both administrators and teachers have important contributions to make. As a teacher who is in over my head with daily instruction, I may lose perspective and need informed help. Likewise, the administrators need to listen to what teachers tell them about what does or does not work and pass that information to their supervisors.

The best change occurs slowly and comes from teachers themselves. It takes longer but it lasts. In the twenty school systems in the state of Maine who showed top scores and exemplary practice in primary reading, the initial vision for excellence was teacher-based and involved only a few local administrators (Graves 2001). The local vision for quality reading instruction was wonderfully supported and funded by Title I, the state, and state universities who designed courses to fit local needs. I looked for other common characteristics, and found these: effective change took from five to eleven years; there was low staff turnover; and heavy investments were made in inservice that emphasized developing local expertise. Although these systems were subject to state assessment, they relied heavily on the data from running records as analyzed by their own teams. One educator expressed it best, "We didn't have a lot of money to throw at the problem, so we had to use our money carefully and what better investment is there than the teachers who had the vision in the first place."

When I taught, I found that if I asked students about their aspirations for learning, those aspirations usually exceeded my own. I suspect that teacher standards are more ambitious than those developed by the officials higher up in the hierarchical chain simply because teachers know best what students are capable of doing.

Are Long, Slow Thinkers an Endangered Species?

As computers get faster, we expect people to keep up with them. Faster is better. The other day I watched a friend with broadband access click on a file; half a blink and the full file appeared on the screen. Three more clicks of her mouse, and she reported information that would have taken me weeks to acquire. I confess that I envied her speed and efficiency. Our computer files have become extensions of our minds.

Bill Gates gives potential Microsoft employees tests to examine quickness of thought. James Gleick in his book *Faster* (1999) writes, "Much of life has become a game show, our fingers perpetually poised above the buzzer. We're either the quick or the dead. To be *quick* it used to be enough merely to be alive. Now we expect repartee and fast response times too."

Gleick juxtaposes his discussion about quick thinkers with one about long thinkers. "One could make an all-star list of slow but effective thinkers. Charles Darwin considered himself too slow-witted to engage in argument. 'I suppose I am a very slow thinker,' he said the year he published *The Origin of Species*. Einstein modestly described himself as a slow thinker." Thomas Jefferson could not engage in argument when his draft of the Declaration of Independence was being debated. But he was able to sustain thought for years through a series of essays concerning the natural rights of humankind that ultimately gave rise to that Declaration. Clearly, many of our social, economic, and technological advances have required long thinkers.

Unfortunately, our current assessments are only interested in the quick thinkers. With the stakes for students, teachers, and school systems thus fixed, we bend our instruction to both raise and identify only one kind of thinker. Given the concurrent erosion of time in the school day, we make haste to teach quickly as well. Virtually all tests are timed, and the only questions supplied are by the testing agency. Long thinkers usually formulate their own questions.

I remember my first encounter with a long thinker. Years ago we had a program in my school whereby students could become specialists in a particular interest. Brian focused on the old whaling industry in the area where he lived. He became the school's in-house expert while pursuing his special interest over a six-month period. He read, interviewed authorities, constructed a ship and whales, and reenacted hunting whales on the stage. Brian provided a vision for other children in the school of what it meant to know a subject well but also helped them recognize that it took months to achieve this vision.

David McCullough speaks not of working *on* a book but *in* a book, totally immersed. What long thinking does so well is to allow children to pass from outside their subjects to the inside where they appreciate what it means to know. Here are a cluster of characteristics often associated with long thinkers:

- *They are problem finders.* They formulate their own questions about the world and then search for answers. Their search usually impels them to acquire a cluster of tools and skills that will help them achieve their goals.

- *They enjoy their own company.* They are at home with their own thoughts and do not often require the company of others to pursue their goals. They will often pull out of a group to be alone with their thoughts. They are not necessarily antisocial, but they do require time alone.

- *They have a sense of play.* In the midst of work they find play, a new way, a novel twist. This sense of play and discovery sustains their long thinking.

- *They are highly focused.* They are able to sustain thought on one project to the exclusion of all else. They get caught up in obsessions and special interests: learning to play an instrument or a piece of music, painting a scene, constructing a mechanism, reading a book, writing a book. They are often unaware of the passing of time.

- *They have been apprenticed to other long thinkers.* They may be fortunate to have a parent, relative, or close friend who is a long thinker and so have witnessed the power of long thinking. Or they may have served a more formal apprenticeship. They may be fortunate enough to have a teacher who is a long thinker and consciously demonstrates long thinking through her own specialized interests, allowing the class to travel with her through the process.

Origins of Long Thinkers

What I am about to tell you is based more on informal observations of the play habits of children age six months through the early teens than on well-documented research. I am convinced that the autodirectedness of play is at the heart of children's abilities to assume longer-thinking roles later in life.

Very small children will focus on an object, selecting a rattle or toy from a field of objects and sustaining interest in it for some time, exploring it kinesthetically, orally, and visually. If being read to by an adult, these children focus on the book to the exclusion of all else in the room. Later, when speech is acquired, a running commentary of egocentric speech accompanies play. In one sense children are developing their own company for later, more extended play situations. There are times when children assemble collections of dolls, stuffed animals, trucks, jets, books, and toy guns. They arrange and rearrange and classify these collections. At some point in their development, children move into deep play, which is more involved, extends over a number of days or weeks or months, and often has a "becoming" nature to it. Children are working out adult roles, making elaborate constructions, and in some cases involving other children as part of the play.

Helping Children Become Long Thinkers

In an era when time is precious and the time for teaching is becoming more and more segmented, it takes a great deal of planning to help children develop their long-thinking abilities. I recommend Camille Allen's book *The Multigenre Research Report* (2001), in which she identifies many entry points into long thinking. She demonstrates her own long thinking on a single project throughout the semester with her university students, who in turn work on projects with children and teachers in the schools. In *Investigate Nonfiction* (1989), although I don't use the term *long thinking,* I talk about *specialty reporting* and discuss ways to help young children develop their special interests over the longer term.

When children see their teacher and especially their classmates engaged in long thinking, they learn to understand its power. Children take on the power of long thinking when they successfully identify areas about which they know a little and want to learn more. They are able to sustain their thinking using a number of resources and skills. It usually takes several tries before children begin to pass from outside their subjects to inside them and experience what successful long-term thinking feels like.

Both quick thinking and long thinking are important skills for the successful learner of the twenty-first century. The Yale psychologist Robert J. Sternberg points out that "the essence of intelligence would seem to be in knowing when to think and act quickly, and knowing when to think and act slowly" (Gleick 1999, 114). Clearly, the issues of our time require sustained, long-term thinking. The long thinker must not be allowed to become an endangered species.

What Writing Does

DEMOCRACIES DEPEND ON THE QUALITY OF THEIR CITIZENS' THINKING. In the midst of some community meeting when arguments are headed in a misguided direction, we hope someone will stand up and say, "No, it would be a mistake to take that tack; here's another way to look at the problem." One of the best ways to develop solid thinkers early on is by asking children to think clearly in writing. Writing, when taught well, establishes knowledgeable territory for the thinker. Learning to write is a slow process that begins in kindergarten and continues through high school and beyond. Unfortunately, with time an ever-decreasing commodity in the school day, writing has been pushed to one side in favor of reading and those other subjects that can be easily tested by computer.

We need to consider seriously how writing can help develop the citizens of tomorrow. Let's take an inside/outside look at how sixth grader Jennifer is learning to think and grow through her writing. Jennifer has struggled with her report on Joan of Arc for two solid weeks. The deadline is approaching, and her report is going nowhere. "Try writing as if you were Joan; write it first person, present tense," Ms. Franzen, her teacher, advises. Later, Jennifer reports on her process: "In one moment I sat there looking at the piece and hating it. I was outside my subject. When I wrote as Joan, I became that person and suddenly I was on the inside living the life of Joan."

Not all writers experience Jennifer's dramatic crossing of the invisible line from outside to inside their subject. But hers is a more universal experience than we might expect. Jennifer has researched her subject but is unable to bring her own voice to bear on the material. When Jennifer passes to the inside, she not only simulates Joan's feelings as a woman but also organizes the material to reflect her own voice. Later, she presents her material to the class as if she were Joan. Finally, her written report leaves the room for the library and is read by other students in her building.

Writing allows Jennifer to get the ideas out of her head and on to the paper. Until her writing reaches the paper, Jennifer doesn't really know what she thinks. Writing gives her the distance she needs to understand her feelings and ideas. When Jennifer writes, she is on the inside looking out; later, as she rereads her work, she is on the outside again, wondering whether the page properly reflects her feelings and her ideas.

Jennifer is learning to be a long, slow thinker through her writing. During her research she reads and thinks rapidly, peripatetically. It's so easy for all of us to skip on the surface of an idea and somehow convince ourselves that we know our topic. Writing allows Jennifer to freeze an image or an idea, ponder it on the page, then build thought upon thought. Gradually, she will learn to sustain thought on a single subject for as long as six weeks to six months.

Jennifer is fortunate to have a teacher who helps her students learn how to reread their own work. Ms. Franzen demonstrates rereading her own first drafts and talks aloud about what she is trying to do in those drafts. She shows her students how she uncovers the possibilities in a draft as she struggles with the one question her piece is about. The most fragile moment for a writer comes at the point of rereading the first draft. But if the writer has had experience looking for the possibilities there, then the process can be a productive experience.

Once Jennifer is invested in her text and is on a genuine search to discover the truth about Joan of Arc, she is not just drafting a text. Rather, she is composing a life, page after page. "Oh, this is what I think," Jennifer says to herself. In learning how to read her draft, she catches a glimmer of an original idea. She is surprised by the feelings of being a young woman who wants to take a position in writing about something important.

Writing also allows Jennifer to consider points of view other than her own. New at testing out other points of view, she nevertheless presses on. In the process of working on her paper she considers the Protestant, or English, point of view and that of the French Catholic. But her search for a point of view doesn't end there. She reasons, "Since I am asking for more demonstrations of courage by women today, I need to consider some modern examples of Catholic women who stepped forward in courage." She also ponders what her girlfriends or, worse, male teenagers may say.

When Jennifer writes she works within three time dimensions. Her actual writing is in the present, going on to the page right now, but once written it becomes history. Writing is an act of self-transcendence. Her Joan of Arc paper prompts Jennifer to wonder, "What kind of woman have I been?" She has a collection of writing in her folder, her personal writer's history. She looks back at her writing as having dealt primarily with trivial issues. On the other hand, Jennifer's piece on Joan of Arc is ultimately showcased in the school library and allows her to transcend herself in time *and* space. She has floated a piece of writing into the future, where others can read and learn about Joan of Arc next week, next month, next year.

Jennifer may even get responses from her readers, some who may not even know her. In this instance writing is a social act connecting and reconnecting her with unknown audiences. Quite suddenly, Jennifer is no longer a person alone but a human being with ideas and emotions connected to others in her room and in her school. She has experienced the miracle of communication.

Writing is an important medium of thought in which each student knows he or she can discover new ideas and express them within a democratic society. When the students in Jennifer's class and countless others like them express their ideas in essays, poetry, and fiction, they gain experience in accepting or debating other points of view, skills essential to the future of a democratic republic.

The Bottom Line

I've enjoyed conversations with many businesspeople over the years. I respect their concerns about education and the marketplace. Below I run into a tough-minded businessman (TB) willing to enter into a respectful exchange of ideas.

DG: Sir, I know you are concerned about performance in the schools. You've gone on record as saying that your company has to show a profit or it would go out of business. That's how you hold your company accountable, annual profits. Stockholders want to see proper dividends, or they'll take their money and invest it where it *will* be profitable. In sum, you believe that schools should be similarly accountable and everyone should stop fussing about all the testing the President is advocating.

TB: You have it partly right. We live in a competitive world, and I don't mean just in this country. My company is up against competition from the Far East—the labor costs in China, Korea, and India are extraordinarily low. We have to push every margin to make a profit. We can't tolerate inefficiency, poor labor practices, or bad management. Everyone from top to bottom expects performance, and we monitor it from day to day. It is only natural that I'd expect the same performance in schools. I want everyone from the board of education to the superintendent to the principal to the teachers to set specific goals that will show that learning is taking place. And test scores should rise gradually each year. I hasten to add that unless we're able to create an intelligent labor force, one that can truly compete in the world market, we're going to lose our number one position.

DG: You seem to put great store in scores. Before we get into that, I'm curious about your hiring practices. When you hire a manager, salesman, or even an assistant in your office, what are you looking for?

TB: Well, I want someone who is smart. That is, they know our line of business. I want them to have skills that are as good as or better than our competitors'. They need to have initiative. I guess I'd call it drive. Next, I want them to be creative, to come up with a different twist to solving problems. They should be able to stand on their own two feet and fight for their ideas. I guess you'd call that conviction. Finally, they need to be team players. There comes a point when you just have be a team player, give up a little ego for the sake of maybe a better idea. And damn it, when they write memos, I don't want any beating about the bush, I just want them to say what they have to say in crisp, direct language. I've got some bozos who have cost our company big money because their memos were too vague.

DG: Have you been able to come up with a test that allows you to identify such a person?

TB: The people down in personnel have tests that they say get at the personality stuff, but I like to look at the track record of the person I want to hire. What have they done? What problems have they solved? I like to throw problems at them in a face-to-face interview to see how they'd go about solving them.

DG: Would you ever select your employees on the basis of a multiple-choice test?

TB: No way! Maybe I could do a little screening that way for some things.

DG: Sir, almost everything you've said about what makes a competent worker is precisely what we want in our students. We prize initiative, drive, the ability to solve problems, and, yes, we want them to be able to stand behind their arguments and beliefs. But, like you, we don't think we can identify the good student using multiple-choice tests. We want them to build up portfolios that show performance in a variety of areas. And more than that, we want to ask them challenging questions about the contents of their portfolios. Further, this is something we'd like the student to prepare for in advance.

TB: That's all well and good, but I don't have much confidence in teachers' ability to pull off something as sophisticated as that. How do I know that one teacher is as competent as the next? I understand there's a huge turnover in teachers right now. You have many, many new ones to hire. How can we trust that they'll be able to handle what you are advocating?

DG: Alas, we can't always trust that, and I suspect you sometimes find yourself in the same boat, hiring basically competent people you feel you (or qualified consultants) can train. When the job market is booming and there's a scarcity of people, you have to offer better salaries to attract good people, and in many cases you have to offer a retraining program. You take people with some basic skills, but you design your own special programs to bring them up to speed. Right now we have an enormous teacher shortage across the country because so many teachers are retiring or are just fed up with the great hordes who have never been teachers themselves but who nevertheless think they know what's wrong with education. So what we have to do is raise salaries and invest more than modest sums in sound programs of teacher preparation. I say sound, because there are a lot of fly-by-night packaged programs out there trying to fill the void. They are very method-centered.

TB: Isn't that good? Isn't there scientific evidence pointing to the right methods to use? Surely, there are time-proven methods that will boost the scores of kids.

DG: There you go, focusing on scores again. Remember, scores aren't the only indicator that good learning has taken place or that you are hiring the best person. Here's a question for you. I assume you have a sales force for your company. How do you prepare them to make a sale?

TB: First, they have to know their product backward and forward. They need to know how to adapt the product to fit the needs of the customer. From the beginning, they have to know the business of the guys they're selling to. They are very sensitive to the needs of the customer, and they move on from there.

DG: So, is there a set method that fits all customers?

TB: God, no. I see where you are going with this, damn it.

DG: What you described before is precisely what teachers ought to be doing when they teach. Let's say they are teaching reading. They have to know as much as possible about teaching reading as a process. But like you said, it all depends on the needs of the customer, in this case the child. In a way teaching is selling. The teacher constantly has to adapt: every kid is different just like every customer is different. I'd say there's an art to selling and there certainly is an art to teaching. More and more kids are turned off to learning through no fault of their own. I once spoke to a doctor who said, "There's a scientific answer to every ailment; the problem is, will you get enough information from the patient to be able to apply the science? And getting that information, getting enough trust from the patient to be able to express what maybe they don't even want to admit to themselves, is where the art comes in." Does that make sense?

TB: This all seems perhaps *too* logical, but I admit you've got me thinking.

What's That For?

ONE OF MY FAVORITE RESEARCH TOOLS IS THE *WHAT'S THAT FOR?* question. I choose a child in the classroom to show me around and explain the various items and procedures in order to get the child's viewpoint about how the room operates. I point to a book and ask, "What's that for?"

"That's a reading book."

"What are reading books for?"

"It's to help you learn to read."

"If it's to help you learn to read, what good is that? Do you think it's good for you to know how to read?"

"Yes, it's fun. I like adventure stories."

That interchange was with a second grader. The question sequence is typical of an *anthropological* line of questioning. Anthropologists want basic answers about the *function* of tools in a society. Further, they want to get a perspective on how people in the culture attach value to the tool or practice.

A student in one of my research courses pointed to papers fifth graders were writing and asked them, "What are these for?" Basically their responses were, "Oh, these; these are for the teacher." Only a few children attached personal value to their papers ("This will help me to be a better writer"). I asked my student to ask the class's teacher the same question about those same papers, "What are these for?" "Oh, these are for the children so they can become more proficient writers. They need the practice." How interesting that each thought the writing was for the other! How can we prepare our children to become proficient in something if we haven't attached a personal sense of functional power to the act?

I remember vividly the day Frank Smith said something to me that changed my entire view of punctuation, grammar, and spelling. He said, "Everything we do when we write is an act of convention so that both you and the next person can understand what you mean." Conventions are agreements between ourselves and our readers. What is so powerful about Frank's statement is that it immediately gets to function. I introduced this concept to two excellent first-grade teachers in a rural New Hampshire school. They changed their approach to conventions from one of rules to one of functional understanding. They showed their students the power of spaces between words, the serial comma, quotation marks, and capital letters. The children kept lists of the conventions they were using—at first inaccurately (although they still got high praise for attempting them) but later to near mastery. By the end of the year these children were well acquainted in practice and understanding with a mean number of twenty-five different conventions.

On another occasion Shirley Brice Heath, emeritus professor from Stanford, posited, "The origin of the essay is the letter." She had carefully researched the origin of the essay and could show quite clearly the functional relationship between letters and essays. That natural evolution provided me with a new insight into how to teach the essay. Using my own writing, I showed my students how letters to friends can be transformed into essays. Shaping an argument to one person in a letter is usually much easier than doing so for a much larger audience in an essay. On the other hand, it is not that difficult to adjust already existing text and diction to reach broader audiences.

As eagerly as we try to help children understand function in terms of personal power, so too we need to help colleagues, administrators, and politicians understand the function of education. In the midst of a meeting about test scores we need to ask, "What are these for?" It may be quite obvious that the tests and the resultant scores are required by state law. But don't let this answer bring a halt to your questions. Keep going: "How does this testing connect with your understanding of what constitutes learning? What do your students' think is the function of the test? Do they connect this with learning, their learning?" Although we may stretch our credibility a bit thin by doing so, we need to give children some understanding of what testing is all about—what is its function? what does it have to do with them?

Consider asking a related question of colleagues or administrators. "We spend so much time teaching reading and writing. Can we arrive at a common understanding of what reading and writing are for?" If we have not internalized the place of literacy in our own lives, we may not be helping children acquire the rich understanding of reading and writing they need for themselves. More and more children can read but choose not to. They join the ranks of the aliterate, the army of children for whom literacy is not an asset and for whom it has no function.

What Happened to Time for Teaching?

THE LENGTH OF THE SCHOOL DAY IS THE SAME TODAY AS IT WAS when I first began teaching, in 1956, the year I got out of the military. Since that time, however, school curriculum has expanded four- or fivefold, interruptions have doubled, more and more children have special needs, and there are more specialists, community groups, and parents clamoring at the classroom door. Worse, assessment requires time equivalent to that spent on two major subjects. Remember, testing is not teaching.

The good news is that our profession is better educated. More than ever we know how to teach children. But what our profession has learned about good learning theory and human development gets bypassed in the rush to meet hurry-up objectives and boost the test scores of our students.

Twenty-three years ago I was on sabbatical leave in Scotland, and our daughter Laura attended school there for the equivalent of our eighth grade. She studied six major subjects, including three sciences, and left for school in the dark at 7:10

in the morning and returned in the dark at 4:30 in the afternoon. Yet she arrived home relaxed, and often picked up a book to read. In fact, she read three times as many books in that year as she read on returning to a very good school for her freshman year of high school.

Laura's school days in Scotland were interspersed with sports, dance, music, and theatre; the hour allowed for lunch included cricket and other sports and activities. When Laura got off the bus in the States at 2:30 P.M. she was ready to put her fist through the wall. She had few breaks, barely time to get to her locker or speak with classmates, and only twenty minutes for lunch. Worse, her independent reading dropped significantly. If Laura felt the pressure of time, her teachers felt the pressure even more.

There is good reason why teachers' eyes narrow when a supervisor speaks of a new addition to the curriculum, another assessment, another planning meeting. Like an accordion file, the day is viewed as ever expandable, ever flexible. Unfortunately, the day is already jammed with issues that need attention and curriculum to teach, and planning time is ever in short supply.

When I was doing research in classrooms, teachers would inevitably tell me about something new and exciting they had tried. I would affirm the new practice, which was usually a good one. But my next question often caught them off guard: "And what did you decide *not* to do?" I reasoned that in order to add something to a full day, they needed to subtract something they had done in the past. I wanted to find out what practices were on the bottom of the deck. After some reflection they could usually identify something that was less important, something they'd been able to integrate, or something the new practice displaced. I then looked to see if there was a corresponding shift in value.

The teaching life is one of constant change and must remain so. New materials and practices require serious consideration. On the other hand, serious negotiation between teachers and administrators is also required:

1. From what we know about learning and children's development, is this new practice merited?
2. In view of the new practice, what will be discontinued?
3. What can and should be kept from the old practice and how will the new and old be integrated?

When I moderate a workshop, I often ask, "Is there any-one in the audience who will retire this year?" Of those who raise their hand I then jokingly inquire, "Will any of you be willing to sacrifice yourselves for the cause this year and when something new is added ask, 'And what will we subtract to make room for it?'" This always gets a laugh, but I find that sensitive administrators are bothered even more than teach-ers are by the addition of new responsibilities and curriculum demands from above.

The compacted school day leads to sacrifices we may not recognize. When there is less time to teach and there are more frequent interruptions, we tend to teach by telling, "covering" a subject with short, snappy lectures. Even though these lec-tures may be well prepared, there's no substitute for show-ing what we mean using our own or others' work. And showing—demonstrating with a text, writing with students, examining student texts, responding to a book in small groups—almost always takes longer.

When I was doing research on book discussions, I noticed that with the press of time, teachers give more attention to plot and less attention to character. What happens becomes more important than the person behind the action. This holds true in all aspects of curriculum even though the *why* of what happens is best explained through the wants and needs of the participants. Of course, these wants and needs are often am-biguous and take more teaching time. I concluded that to bypass character also means bypassing the student who is struggling to grow up and make his or her own decisions.

If you're a teacher, analyze how much time you actually spend teaching in a three-day period. See how many real teaching minutes you can record each day. We know that straight uninterrupted teaching time is the most effective, so in addition, put an asterisk (*) whenever you are interrupted within (w) or from outside (o) the room. If you're an administrator, spend a little time in teachers' rooms noting how much straight uninterrupted teaching goes on. Then pull grade-level teachers together to discuss how they use their time, how they handle interruptions, and how these things affect the quality of their teaching.

One of the serious casualties of the high-paced day is listening—to children, to colleagues, and to ourselves. I know I'm in trouble when I find that I'm trying to confer with one student while wondering why a student twelve feet away looks so distracted. My eye contact is weak, I'm looking past the face of the student before me, I am rarely in the "now." Life seems to be the next, the next, the next.

The hyperactive day stuffed with activity can make serious inroads on discovery and process, on learning how to apply the tools of learning. Each curriculum area ought to be a laboratory in which students engage with the environment and discover more lasting principles in the discipline. Using discovery and process in reading, math, writing, science, and social studies requires larger blocks of time.

Real teaching time, in which we show our students how to discover and reflect, is in short supply and has been eroding for some time. I find that the less time I have, the more I attempt to do everything on my lists. I am too busy to examine how my time is being used. Am I rushing frenetically from minute to minute without considering what I should *not* do in order to leave myself more quality time? We are in charge, and we need to help and support one another as we make changes for the sake of the bottom line, learning that lasts.

Teaching When Time Is in Short Supply

WE HAD A SECRETARY AT THE UNIVERSITY WHO WAS ASSIGNED TO three professors. Invariably, one of us would stomp into her office, slap some papers on her desk, and mutter, "Got to have this by ten o'clock this morning." Fed up with our urgent demands, especially when they all arrived at once, she purchased a sign at a local stationer's and displayed it prominently on her desk. The sign read, "A Crisis in Your Life Doesn't Necessarily Mean There's a Crisis in Mine," and she had a personality that matched it. When one of us arrived holding papers, before we'd get halfway across the office floor, she'd smile and point to the sign. We three professors got educated in a hurry.

The problem with most school demands is that they are accompanied by an aura of crisis, and we stop thinking. They distract us from attending to sound, well-timed instruction. The sideshow of crisis and interruption can make us forget the main event, teaching and learning. (There are crises that do need to be dealt with. A child who is ill, lost, upset emotionally, or hungry must be attended to.)

Time may be in short supply, but we are in charge of what is left to us. We can choose to turn our backs on the air of crisis that often surrounds us. It is up to us to apply those practices that will in fact result in better learning. We can't remain passive when distractions attempt to make inroads on our instructional time. The bottom line has to be children's learning, learning that lasts. We must continually call attention to uses of time, both those that enhance learning and those that steal from it.

Before any considerations of instructional practices that may save time, my first focus is on the children. Children need to know that as human beings they are more important than what I have to teach them. It is too easy to slip into the trap of attaching moral and existential goodness to learning. "Wonderful child; she's such a good reader." It is easy to like the bright students; I remember searching students' eyes for confirmation that learning in my classroom was an exciting adventure. I needed "the look," and bright students, those eager to please, knew how to give it. Of course, there were other students who didn't care and stared out the window, and still others who showed their distaste for and avoidance of my teaching more aggressively. Quite possibly, I was wasting those students' time.

Knowing children begins with learning their names, preferably *before* the first class. I enter the room eager to match faces and names. I may even take a photo of the class and use that to help me attach names to faces. Of course, names carry with them all sorts of history, ethnicity, and family background. Names have stories behind them. I might ask, "Tell me the story behind your name." Usually that information helps me remember facts about students more easily. I move from knowing their names to knowing what kind of learners they are, what special abilities they have, what their stories are. Finally, I try to confirm this knowledge with them. "I noticed that you are reading *x*. How do you like it?" "I noticed that you hit a home run at recess." (See Graves 2001, 26–27, for a more detailed description of this exercise.)

Noticing is at the heart of building understanding that lasts. If children feel they are known as more than just a grade in a book, they listen differently.

Knowing children is important. But nearly as important is knowing our craft, in whatever discipline we wish to apply it. Nancie Atwell's student B. J. struggled to write a first-person narrative about leaving his mother to go and live with his father. Trying to be accurate in the grip of very complex emotions, B. J. had a hard time getting off the ground. Nancie said, "B. J., try writing this as fiction." That simple switch allowed B. J. some much needed distance. His fictional account gave him more understanding than the personal narrative had. Nancie said, "I learned something from B. J. I learned that the key to writing is to put the right genre between yourself and your objective." Using her knowledge of B. J. and his need of the moment, as well as her long experience with the craft of writing, Nancie achieves exemplary teaching.

Nancie also writes with her students. This is a great time-saver. The students witness the scientist, the teacher, in the laboratory. As Nancie writes, she invites her students into the process and explains what she is doing and why she is doing it. When schools bring me in to spend just an hour with their teachers, I rarely talk but immediately have everyone write, and I write with them. As I write on the overhead, I talk about the process and about various teachers and students with whom I have worked. What both Nancie and I are doing is trying to show where excitement and discovery originate as we talk aloud about the piece. We demonstrate how we listen to our own words on the page. Of course, we invite questions as we go. *What do you wonder about here?*

When in doubt, ask your students for solutions. This is another great time-saver. When children sense that the question is an honest one and the teacher doesn't know the answer, they will exercise knowledge we simply don't possess. I once directed five reading centers, and our screening procedures included one battery of assessments after another. Three years into my work it occurred to me that we never asked the students what they thought their reading problems were. Even if the child's diagnosis is wrong, it shows where the child thinks the problem lies. Most important, we can learn much about the child's feelings when talking about the issues. *And how does that make you feel?* In a flash I could see how much time we'd wasted in the way we'd dealt with some of our tougher cases.

I know no greater time-saver than helping students evaluate their own work. Yes, it takes time to save time. Students spend 95 percent of their time alone with their work. I need to help them acquire the skill to be able to reread their own work critically, but I do so with the certain knowledge that rereading will result in better work.

If students are writing, reading, or doing math only two or three days a week, however, teaching them to examine their work critically won't be as successful. Students who work sporadically in the disciplines are not interested in their products in the same way that students who read and write regularly are. When students write each day on topics they've chosen themselves, they tend to think about their work even when they aren't writing. When they do sit down to write, the topic is already in motion. Miss a day, and it's as if they are starting a book or paper all over again, especially when the children are very young.

We need to take greater charge of our teaching time. When there is an erosion of instructional time, we need to enlist the help of our colleagues in pointing out how instructional time is wasted. Learning to save time requires a lifetime of learning. We need to ask our colleagues directly, *How do you save time, yet still challenge your students? What do your students handle independently that you used to do yourself?* We teach in a time of tension and intimidation, one crisis after another invoked from without. People who are constantly crying, "Crisis!" are overly focused on a dark future.

They fear some day of reckoning and forgo instruction that needs to be attended to today. Expert teachers turn away from the crisis mentality and focus on the teachable moment with the individual child.

The Energy of Continual Composition

I WAS IN DESPAIR. I HAD FOUR DAYS LEFT TO REPORT MY FINDINGS TO the National Institute of Education on the large volume of data from our three-year study of children's writing. I'd worked and worked on the findings and could show general developmental trends in each of our subjects. But when I pressed in more closely, examining the more advanced writers and their process of revision, the data showed that most of them rehearsed before they wrote but they all rehearsed differently. Some drew, some chatted, others wrote notes.

I sat in my study and looked up at the house of my neighbor, Jim, a pomologist at the University, and an expert on fruit trees. I thought about his discipline as a researcher and recalled a stroll and chat in his yard the previous summer. Jim had a quiet way of displaying what he knew. He could look at a tree, not just fruit trees, and tell its story through its growth anomalies, branching, canopy, or disease characteristics. I wondered, "How does Jim do that?" I could smell an answer in the air. (Sometimes researchers sense they are in the presence of an answer, that just a little more thinking will break the problem wide open.) It struck me that Jim could speak about individual trees so concisely because he knew so much data about trees in general; he could apply those data to any given tree.

I went back to pondering my own research question. Minutes later it dawned on me that ultimately the purpose of all research about humans is to reveal our differences. I could take all the data we'd learned from our study and others like it and show how they were manifested differently in individual children. For example, the more advanced children embedded, on average, six or seven different concepts about writing in their descriptions of a piece they'd composed. But each selected different clusters of concepts, thus displaying their individual sensibilities and voice. That finding allowed me to show general classifications of our data that were real contributions in their own right. Since ultimately we all teach individuals within groups, that's where our data could be applied more accurately.

Perhaps my desperation to find an answer to my research dilemma made me widen my search. But continual composing, searching, questioning, reaching for a story, a metaphor, a line, delivered the main insight that helped me report my data successfully. I have to be sure to allow information to flow freely between compartments or categories I may have artificially constructed. I've come to understand that these types of activities are part of the act of *continual composition*. While we compose we try to connect disparate understanding, like connecting what we've observed about fruit trees to what we see in humans.

In her speech accepting the Nobel laureate in poetry, Wyslawa Zymborska said that she could tell a dying society or institution by its use of adverbs. The more absolute the adverb, such as *never* and *always,* the more authoritative, contained, and brittle the institution. She showed how highly orthodox societies like fascism and communism control their people through highly inflexible, absolutist language. Her simple statement led me to look at children's adverbs differently. (I also learned, as many writers have, that adverbs are often used to prop up weak verbs.)

Writing is my laboratory for thinking. Writing allows me to put two ideas side by side on a page and make them hold still. They may be racing in my mind, but on the page I can examine them in juxtaposition, until my mind races off again, pursuing the sparks that have jumped between them. The sparks are caused by questions. I remember a chance remark by Michael, one of the seven-year-olds in my first study of children's writing. I had written in my field notes, "You know, Mr. Graves, you like the writing, but I like the drawing." Michael's large twelve-by-eighteen-inch piece of paper had a much larger space at the top for drawing than the lines allotted at the bottom for his writing, but he perceptively observed that I'd only asked questions about his writing. I'd ignored his drawing. Energy jumped between those two words in my field notes, *writing* and *drawing*. I'd placed a wall between writing and drawing in my study design. I had to take down that wall and study their relationship if I was to understand writing. When I did a step-by-step analysis of Michael's drawing I realized that he was right, his drawing contained far more information than his writing. I subsequently did schematics of both texts to show their structure and relative importance to the thinking process.

New structures, new insights, can come from chance remarks by friends or from a line in a book. When we compose, we're always ready to expand a remark into a major idea or use it to answer a long-nagging question.

One of the chief ways to prompt exciting thinking and theorizing is to trust the shadows. I've learned that most solutions are not found by keeping to the obvious, the straightforward road. Rather, they lie in the shadows. I find more ideas and theories in my writing when I let in peripheral ideas. When I first begin writing, I let everything and anything in, coaxing out whatever may be lurking in the bushes. I don't put up any walls. Once I have an array of thoughts and ideas,

I look for connections that may be triggered by a line, a word, or a simple statement. One word may suggest an entire story. Most of the time, of course, there are *no* connections. I joke with friends about my "dump picking." Rummage long enough in the trash, however, and you'll walk home from the dump carrying a real trophy.

One of the byproducts of the state of continual composition is a hunger for good theory. Theories are the ultimate connectors, and they usually reside in simple statements. Neil Simon has said, "Nothing happens in my plays until the main character wants something and wants it badly." I connected that statement to another idea expressed by professional writers, "Character is all." Plot comes from what the main character wants. Indeed, there are no mountains, storm clouds, or magnificent sunsets unless *someone sees them.* James Carroll developed Simon's theory by observing that when a character wants something badly, the force behind this wanting usually produces a choice and often opposition. Story carries these events forward to resolution or paradox. I've applied these theories to the study of characters in history, science, art, and biography in my book *Bring Life into Learning* (1999). A quick question to a child—*What does your character want?*—directs him immediately to the heart of a book or a piece of fiction.

Story is the engine of continual composition, variables interacting around a central theme or theory. Stories show humans in context and complex variables in interaction. After finishing *Bring Life into Learning,* I began to be bothered by how much fatigue and stress I'd been seeing in the teaching profession. In the last five hundred yards of a five-mile run with a friend, a question came to mind that gave me a way to study this very complex issue: *Tell me, what gives you energy, takes it away, and for you is a waste of time?* That simple question was the focus of my life for the next eighteen months and gave rise to *The Energy to Teach.*

The state of continual composition is one of relentless questioning, looking for stories, listening for answers in what people say, and exploring data to arrive at theories. This continual composing allows no walls between disparate pieces of information. Rather, this night-and-day composition becomes a natural part of living, as one theory after another is developed and discarded. Its chief laboratory is writing, where thinking is slowed down and ideas are juxtaposed in interesting combinations. There is much energy in this life of constant exploration and discovery. Something new and wonderful is usually just around the next bend.

A Mutual Trust

A GOOD FRIEND ONCE PLAYED A PAINFUL TRICK ON ME. SINCE WE didn't have kindergartens in our school system, all incoming first graders were given the Metropolitan Readiness test. Those children who did poorly were enrolled in a special readiness class. Our eldest child, Marion, was slated for first grade in the fall and took the test. Marion knew some letters and words, enjoyed books, and seemed a bright child. That she might do poorly never entered my mind. But my friend, the elementary supervisor, called me into her office, asked me to sit down, and with grave tones explained to me that Marion did poorly on the Metropolitan. I think she used the word *flunked*. When she saw the look of devastation on my face, she immediately recanted and said she was only joking.

But I had spent ten seconds feeling what most parents feel at such news: an emotion-laden mixture of depression and disillusionment. How could I have been so wrong about a child I had seen as intelligent in my own household? I had answered Marion's questions, read books to her, and participated in her joy at learning new things. Marion loved birds and wildlife and seemed to have an exploratory nature.

Most parents witness wonderful acts of intelligence in their children and share these success stories with grandparents, aunts, uncles, the next-door neighbors. On the other hand, some parents have had struggles of their own when they were in school, or they come from another culture, and they worry that their children will not do well. Still other children are abused, ill fed, and suffer physical and emotional problems. All of these children can be in the same classroom.

Remarkable things can happen when wise teachers both believe in and skillfully expect more from their students. Some thirty years ago a team of researchers set out to study intelligence in the city of Montreal (Pederson, Faucher, and Eaton 1978). Their research centered on the question, *how stable is IQ over time?* They examined city records encompassing many years. During their study they identified a first-grade teacher, Miss A, who taught in a lower-socioeconomic section of Montreal and whose students consistently scored higher IQs than other first graders in the city. Further, these children maintained their high IQ scores throughout their school careers.

The researchers put their original research question aside and explored the phenomenon of this first-grade teacher, locating the now-grown-up adults who had been in her classes. When interviewed, these people vividly remembered Miss A's firm belief in their abilities. And that belief had led many of them to become prominent professionals now very much involved in their communities. (Miss A's influence was so great that other adults the researchers spoke with were sure they had had her when in fact they hadn't.)

A better-known study, *Pygmalion in the Classroom*, conducted in San Francisco, manipulated the grouping of junior high school students. A group of randomly selected students were told that they had unusual intellectual abilities that had been previously overlooked. From then on they were treated as if they had this new intelligence. The study results showed that their performance significantly changed for the better.

I mention these two studies to show that parents often intuit the nascent abilities in their children. They may not be able to summon the words to articulate what they've seen but sense that what their child is able to do in the home has not been revealed in school. The central question is, *what can schools and parents do together to reveal the precious potential that is in every child?*

Teachers and parents have the everlasting problem of finding the time to talk with one another. We all lead very busy lives. In most cases, both members of a couple work, and finding a way to be in contact with their children's school and teachers is very difficult. Single-parent households are even more pressured. However, more and more parents are connected to the Internet and have email addresses, and most teachers and administrators have their own voice-mailboxes. (You may wish to consider the additional contact suggestions presented in the parent chapter in *The Energy to Teach*, Graves 2001.)

I've noticed that top teachers have no difficulty maintaining strong relationships with parents. Effective relationships between teacher and parent have three characteristics:

1. The teacher views the parent as a partner in educating the child.
2. Collections of the child's work are maintained that allow both teacher and parent to view progress.
3. Specific information is shared about and between home and school.

I've been on both sides of the parent-teacher meeting. I chuckle as I acknowledge the attitude in the back of my mind in each case, two versions of the same question: *Will she think I am a good teacher? Will he think I am a good parent?* Both versions are laden with emotion, and in some way, directly or indirectly, both will be answered in the course of the year.

Teachers and parents need to exchange the vision they have of and for the child. I as teacher need to recognize that

I am but one of many teachers the child will have in her journey through life. The parent, on the other hand, is likely the one constant in that child's life. From the outset I have to view the parent as a very important co-educator. I have questions for the parent: *Tell me about your child when she plays alone, when she plays with others. Is there a special place where your child plays in the house? outside? Tell me about the responsibilities your child has at home. Would you tell me about something you have taught or showed your child how to do? Tell me about things your child may make, put together, paint, about books he may read or pick up.* Obviously, not all of these questions can be handled in one session.

Meetings with parents should center around collections of work. (If work is sent home piecemeal, then the child, teacher, and parent won't be able to see the trajectory of progress. A parent should be able to take his or her child's portfolio home at any point to examine it, but the work needs to be back the next day to be used in class.) One element of the parent-teacher meeting should be the teacher asking parents what they see in the work. Maybe the parent will be reminded of some of the child's interests, something she knows more about. One of the best places to note both progress and background information is the child's own writing. When children choose what they write about and the genre they will use, parents often have helpful moments of recognition: "Oh, this is about our trip to the Museum of Natural History. Did you know that Andrea is interested in prehistoric animals?" Collections also allow teachers to spread out pieces of work written over a period of time, to present them in chronological order and ask, "Do you see any changes here from the beginning of the month to the end? What concerns do you have?"

Collections of work also allow the teacher to be specific about progress. She can move in more closely to the material and show where the details of learning are occurring: "See here how Billy's use of capitalization has improved." "This topic is a new one, and it took real courage for him to break from some of the very safe things he'd written about before." I like to share with parents the notes I've taken about a child's ability to evaluate his own work.

Both parents and teachers have a vision for the child, and the child is already shaping his or her own vision of learning and life. Parents, children, and teachers all have information—detailed, emotional, and visionary—that they all need to understand. The good conference ends with a joint understanding of what will be required to realize our respective visions for this child, this year and in the future.

Children go to school 180 days out of 365, not quite half the calendar year. During a 24-hour day, the school has them 6.5 hours. For 17.5 hours they attend other "schools," whether at home or in the community. Because for better or worse, learning does continue when the child is not in the formal classroom. Both parents and teachers need to be more acquainted with all the schools the child attends.

Building an Energy-Filled
Future for Public Education

IF PUBLIC EDUCATION IS TO SUCCEED IN ITS MISSION, IT MUST RETHINK its relationship to fundamental principles. We must rethink our way of learning from students in order to teach better. Local innovation and vision must take precedence over top-down attempts to standardize improvement. Parents have to assume more responsibility for the education of their children, and public education must help them do so. We have to think of quality education for all of our citizens, not just some. In short, we need to get back to thoughtfulness (Brown 1991), in terms of both our own rich, provocative thinking and a respect for the thinking of others.

We need to look at student potential through a different lens. We have to look at the diversity of children's intelligence and teach them about learning through the things they do well. More immigrants entered America in the nineties than in any other decade in our history. We must take advantage of their cultural gifts and learn from them. Not only will this enrich our culture, but our respect for what they bring to us will help *them* learn. Unfortunately, we currently see our students through the gimlet eye of reading performance alone. Reading is important and does contribute to success in learning. However, reading exists for the child, not the child for the reading score.

Enormous, diverse potential lies in every child. Neurophysiologists continually point to the brain's enormous potential and to its million billion connections, or synapses (Edelman and Tononi 2000). Only a small percentage of the brain is ever used. Howard Gardner's work unfolds the diversity of human intelligence, as does Vera John Steiner's book *Notebooks of the Mind.*

As important as the mind are the emotions. Emotions are the engine of the intellect. When we attend to a child's emotions, we are looking at what the child wants. We need to acknowledge those desires and help children understand them, allow them to capture a vision of what is possible in their life. Teachers who teach well evoke emotions that are more than skin deep. That is, the child knows the teacher sees something of great worth in her. She is reminded that she has great potential because she sees this sense of potential written on her teacher's face.

Children are the future of this country. Ask the marketers who invest enormous sums of money in advertising products for children to buy. They know they need to teach children early to buy what they want them to buy. My research over the past thirty years has convinced me that we have underestimated what children can do. Linda Rief, middle school teacher in Durham, New Hampshire, has shown us that her middle school students are capable of rereading their work as well as any outstanding teacher of writing, in some cases as well as professional writers.

We have gotten evaluation backwards. Far more time needs to be spent in *showing children how* to evaluate their work. Good teachers like Mary Ellen Giacobbe, Pat McLure, Virginia Secor, Sharon Taberski, Penny Kittle, Paula Rogovin, Tom Romano, and James Burke show us again and again the wonderful work that results when teachers have high expectations for their students. Their students have a personal, emotional investment in what they do because the work is closely related to what they want to become. In short, they can articulate the function and purpose of what they are doing for themselves.

We have to regain a sense of our students' potential by purposefully looking through their eyes at the world around them. This, of course, is easy to say but difficult to do. I often conduct a demonstration with about ten students. I assign three teachers to each student. Thus, there are about thirty teachers in the room, in teams of three. As I teach, the observers' task is to record everything their student does, writes, says, or sees in the course of my teaching. When the demonstration is over, I tell the teachers to pool their observations and then interpret the data as if they are the child they watched. I also ask another question: "What could I have done to help build this group into a more effective learning community?" Such training must continue for all teachers, just as medical people have to undergo continued, detailed training and assessment.

As much as our future lies in our children, it also lies in their teachers. Our top teachers take an unwavering stance of expectation. Their faces reflect the potential they see in student work. They work tirelessly to get the student to experience that same sense of potential. At some point all these outstanding teachers were beginners themselves. Just about every research study I've done or read shows it is the teacher who makes the greatest difference. Method is secondary. We need to know how to recognize rich potential in our future teachers.

This is what I look for:

- *They have ideals.* They have a vision of the possible, and their history reflects strong ethical concerns. They place their loyalty in an enduring tradition, a wisdom that survives the passage of time (Gardner, Csikszentmihalyi, and Damon, *Good Work*, 2001).

- *They enjoy children, young people, and people in general.* Mining their past, they tell stories about their best friends, their parents, other relatives, their children. They have a language with which to talk about people. If they have taught, they can speak about what they have learned from children.

- *They demonstrate a capacity for learning.* They enjoy learning new things and can speak about the process of how they learned with some objectivity. They talk about teachers from their past, in school and out, giving us a glimpse of the kind of teacher they wish to become. They talk about the books they are reading, and they have a portfolio of recent writing and thinking. The teacher has to be the chief learner in the classroom.

We need to build a better future for the profession by allowing teachers to come together in quality circles where they can discuss failures, successes, and issues. The field of medicine is already doing this. Physicians share their failures with one another in order to learn from those failures so they are not repeated. Every teacher knows the burden of students they cannot reach or have taught incorrectly. I am convinced by the data in *The Energy to Teach* (Graves 2001) that many teachers carry overwhelming emotional burdens. New teachers especially need to be able to share the emotional aspects of teaching.

When I investigated lasting change in top Maine school systems (Graves 2001), it struck me that it was brought about by bottom-up strategies beginning with teachers and a few local administrators. Working together, they brought their visions to the state department of education and lobbied state universities to design courses to help them accomplish their designs. Best of all, they made large investments in teacher inservice, avoiding sweeping mandates of particular methods and encouraging multiple approaches reflecting child and teacher diversity. In short, this was high-quality American democracy in action. I was also struck by the high energy evident in these school systems and by the quality of their students' work. More states need to recapture the energy that pours from teachers when the vision they are trying to fulfill is theirs.

Parents and teachers have an important stake in their children's future. I have witnessed the great energy of parents and teachers working together at the Manhattan New School (Harwayne, *Going Public,* 1999). I have seen the marvelous work in Paula Rogovin's first-grade class (*Classroom Interviews,* 1998) as the children learn to read and write by examining their family history and occupations, their neighborhoods, their rich native cultures. We need to capitalize on what parents know and show them how their contributions are useful within the classroom. When parents feel they are part of the education of their children they see more clearly how they can help. More important, when parents are invited in, we learn so much more about them that they can use to help their children.

I end with a call to challenge current uses of assessment. Under the guise of objectivity and accountability, these assessments lower standards for our learners. Worse, they fail to challenge them. Our students are not asked to produce good short- and long-term thinking. They are not asked to design, create, or write to show their ability to think convincingly. We must provide a new assessment design that results in greater challenge to both teachers and students. Further, qualitative data should be supplied to show evidence of initiative and intrinsic motivation. Until such alternative measures are in effect, current defective measures will continue to run rampant, the hunger for numbers unabated.

Current approaches to teaching in many parts of the country emphasize methodologies based on "scientific" data. State standards that mandate "correct" methods or singular methodologies that emphasize skill and drill at the expense of children's thinking bypass children and they bypass their teachers, who must be responsive to the learning of these particular children in this particular time and place.

Strangely, with all the emphasis on good scores, we rarely hear any mention of children learning to think. When teachers administer skill-and-drill methodologies unthinkingly, their own intellectual abilities and judgments are seriously affected. But when they focus on what a child knows, they begin to see the potential in their own thinking. Thinking and a respect for others' thinking is the foundation of our democracy.

That No Child May Be Left Behind
A Modern Parable on Public Education

ONE SATURDAY WHEN I WAS ABOUT ELEVEN YEARS OLD OUR BOY Scout patrol, the Wolf Patrol, set out to climb a mountain. Our young adult leader kept repeating, "Now don't fall behind, because if you do you might get lost. You could make a wrong turn, lose your way, and we'd have to send out a search party for you." His tone carried an edge suggesting severe embarrassment to anyone who might be foolish enough to lag behind.

Our leader was a grim-faced young man nine or ten years older than we were. He barked orders like a master sergeant. "All right, let's go over the list. Double-check these: canteen, hiking stick, first-aid kit, ace bandage for sprains, compass, scout knife, extra clothing, poncho. You never know when you'll get a sudden change in the weather." His tone implied a disaster lurking around every turn. I had everything on the list. I knew I'd be relieved when this hike was completed. We stood there waiting and obedient, a group of individuals, some of us afraid we wouldn't measure up and would drag the rest of the patrol down with us.

I had the feeling our leader didn't really enjoy what he was doing. Perhaps this was his first crack at this sort of leadership and he felt enormous responsibility for so many less experienced young scouts. He certainly seemed anxious about the unexpected. He was probably fulfilling a leadership requirement, just as we were checking off one more experience on the list to advance in rank.

I was the smallest and lightest member of the patrol. My legs were short, the pack heavy. I remember we didn't talk much as we went up the mountain single file. It wasn't long before I was at the back of the pack. When the patrol went around a bend, I feared that when I got to the turn the group would have disappeared. I carefully checked the blazes on the trees, but sometimes the distance from one blaze to the next was a bit too far and a queasy knot grew in my stomach. My eyes never wavered from the trail or the blazes. And that's about all I remember about the hike. I remember no joy at the summit, only relief. Our leader said little, and I suspect he was surprised that we'd all arrived without incident.

Three years later, just before I turned fourteen, I had to take another hike, up a mountain 1500 feet higher than the first. It was on our list of required experiences, and I did not look forward to the prospect.

This time we had a more experienced leader, a young family man in his mid-thirties. He held one meeting prior to the day of the climb to review equipment and our preparation. He gave a new interpretation to our required list of implements. His attitude was one of opportunity, the joy of meeting new challenges. Above all he stressed teamwork. We took our ace bandages and practiced wrapping sprained ankles, reviewed different carries for anyone no longer able to walk. Should anyone be injured, we would rotate the portage teams to save our energy. He told stories about crossing brooks and rivers. He spoke of the birds that liked water and could lead us to it and about the raptors we'd encounter once we crossed the timberline. He had a map indicating the best views and waterfalls.

During his explanations he recounted disasters he had experienced. Once he made a leap from a boulder with a full bladder and wet his pants. He foolishly tried to tightrope a narrow log and fell into a river. How we laughed as he acted out his balancing act. Another time he forgot his canteen. This was more serious. Another person had a backup canteen and shared it with him. Our strategy would be to give anyone low on water short measures from everyone else's canteen.

On the day of the hike, we were all paired off with hiking buddies. I didn't realize it at the time, but looking back I see that he chose the two strongest hikers to be the sweeps. Their job was to bring up the rear, look for anything someone might drop, check whether any part of the trail might need repair, and monitor the blazes, making sure none were missed at critical junctures. If anyone was injured or fell behind, the sweeps were to make sure these slower hikers arrived safely at the summit.

We sat around at each stop and shared what we had seen since the last resting point. Our leader then described what we might expect before we reached the next resting point. He made sure that each of us had a chance to speak. I also recall his close observations of each member. "You've got a strap that's ready to let go, Timmy." "Wally, that jacket is going to make you sweat. Sometimes being too hot from sweat can translate into cold at higher altitudes. You have a fresh shirt inside your pack, right?" Because of this wonderful leader (I think his name was Herb), I've enjoyed hiking ever since.

We arrived at the summit giddy with excitement and accomplishment. I remember looking down a rock face and thinking I'd never seen a view like this. I was aware of new feelings I needed to explore. We began to discuss other peaks we might climb. And of course we thought we had done it all ourselves. Nothing could stop us!

References

Allen, Camille. 2001. *The Multigenre Research Paper: Voice, Passion, and Discovery in Grades 4–6.* Portsmouth, NH: Heinemann.

Atwell, Nancie. 1998. *In the Middle.* 2d ed. Portsmouth, NH: Boynton/Cook.

Berliner, David, and Bruce J. Biddle. 1995. *The Manufactured Crisis: Myths, Fraud, and the Attack on America's Public Schools.* Boston: Addison-Wesley.

Brown, Rexford. 1991. *Schools of Thought.* San Francisco: Jossey-Bass.

Edelman, Gerald, and Giulio Tononi. 2000. *A Universe of Consciousness: How Matter Becomes Imagination.* New York: HarperCollins.

Gardner, Howard, Mihaly Csikszentmihalyi, and William Damon. 2001. *Good Work.* New York: Basics Books.

Gleick, James. 1999. *Faster: The Acceleration of Just About Everything.* New York: Pantheon.

Graves, Donald H. 2001. *The Energy to Teach.* Portsmouth, NH: Heinemann.

————. 1999. *Bring Life into Learning*. Portsmouth, NH: Heinemann.

————. 1995. *A Fresh Look at Writing*. Portsmouth, NH: Heinemann.

————. 1989. *Investigate Nonfiction*. Portsmouth, NH: Heinemann.

————. 1978. *Balance the Basics: Let Them Write*. New York: The Ford Foundation.

Harwayne, Shelley. 1999. *Going Public*. Portsmouth, NH: Heinemann.

Jackson, Phil. 1995. *Sacred Hoops*. New York: Hyperion.

Lipsett, Seymour. 1996. *American Exceptionalism: A Double-Edged Sword*. New York: W. W. Norton.

McQuillan, Jeff. 1998. *The Literacy Crisis: False Claims, Real Solutions*. Portsmouth, NH: Heinemann.

National Conference on Excellence in Education. 1983. *A Nation at Risk: The Imperative for Educational Reform*. Washington, DC: U.S. Department of Education.

Ohanian, Susan. 2000. *One Size Fits Few: The Folly of Educational Standards*. Portsmouth, NH: Heinemann.

Pedersen, Eigil, Therese Annette Faucher, and William Eaton. 1978. "A New Perspective on the Effects of First-Grade Teachers on Children's Subsequent Adult Status." *Harvard Educational Review* 48 (1).

Rogovin, Paula. 1998. *Classroom Interviews*. Portsmouth NH: Heinemann.

Rosenthal, Robert, and Lenore Jacobsen. 1968. *Pygmalion in the Classroom*. New York: Holt, Rinehart & Winston.

Steiner, Vera John. 1985. *Notebooks of the Mind*. Albuquerque: University of New Mexico Press.

Thomas, Lewis. 1979. *The Medusa and the Snail: More Notes of a Biology Watcher*. New York: Viking.